FAIRY TALE

This volume offers a comprehensive, critical and theoretical introduction to the genre of the fairy tale. It:

- explores the ways in which folklorists have defined the genre
- assesses the various methodologies used in the analysis and interpretation of fairy tale
- provides a detailed account of the historical development of the fairy tale as a literary form
- engages with the major ideological controversies that have shaped critical and creative approaches to fairy tales in the twentieth and twenty-first centuries
- demonstrates that the fairy tale is a highly metamorphic genre that has flourished in diverse media, including oral tradition, literature, film and the visual arts.

A clear and illuminating guide, *Fairy Tale* offers an essential resource for the field.

Andrew Teverson is Director of Studies for English Literature and Creative Writing at Kingston University London, UK. He is author of *Salman Rushdie* (2007).

THE NEW CRITICAL IDIOM

SERIES EDITOR: JOHN DRAKAKIS, UNIVERSITY OF STIRLING

The New Critical Idiom is an invaluable series of introductory guides to today's critical terminology. Each book:

- provides a handy, explanatory guide to the use (and abuse) of the term;
- offers an original and distinctive overview by a leading literary and cultural critic;
- relates the term to the larger field of cultural representation.

With a strong emphasis on clarity, lively debate and the widest possible breadth of examples, *The New Critical Idiom* is an indispensable approach to key topics in literary studies.

Also available in this series:

The Author by *Andrew Bennett*
Autobiography – *second edition by Linda Anderson*
Adaptation and Appropriation by *Julie Sanders*
Allegory by *Jeremy Tambling*
Class by *Gary Day*
Colonialism/Postcolonialism – *second edition by Ania Loomba*
Comedy by *Andrew Stott*
Crime Fiction by *John Scaggs*
Culture/Metaculture by *Francis Mulhern*
Dialogue by *Peter Womack*
Difference by *Mark Currie*
Discourse – *second edition by Sara Mills*
Drama/Theatre/Performance by *Simon Shepherd and Mick Wallis*
Dramatic Monologue by *Glennis Byron*
Ecocriticism – *second edition by Greg Garrard*
Elegy by *David Kennedy*
Epic by *Paul Innes*
Fairy Tale by *Andrew Teverson*
Genders – *second edition by David Glover and Cora Kaplan*
Genre by *John Frow*
Gothic by *Fred Botting*
The Historical Novel by *Jerome de Groot*
Historicism – *second edition by Paul Hamilton*
Humanism – *second edition by Tony Davies*
Ideology – *second edition by David Hawkes*
Interdisciplinarity – *second edition by Joe Moran*

Intertextuality – *second edition by Graham Allen*
Irony by *Claire Colebrook*
Literature by *Peter Widdowson*
Lyric by *Scott Brewster*
Magic(al) Realism by *Maggie Ann Bowers*
Memory by *Anne Whitehead*
Metaphor by *David Punter*
Metre, Rhythm and Verse Form by *Philip Hobsbaum*
Mimesis by *Matthew Potolsky*
Modernism – *second edition by Peter Childs*
Myth – *second edition by Laurence Coupe*
Narrative by *Paul Cobley*
Parody by *Simon Dentith*
Pastoral by *Terry Gifford*
Performativity by *James Loxley*
The Postmodern by *Simon Malpas*
Realism by *Pam Morris*
Rhetoric by *Jennifer Richards*
Romance by *Barbara Fuchs*
Romanticism – *second edition by Aidan Day*
Science Fiction – *second edition by Adam Roberts*
Sexuality – *second edition by Joseph Bristow*
Spatiality by *Robert T. Tally Jr*
Stylistics by *Richard Bradford*
Subjectivity by *Donald E. Hall*
The Sublime by *Philip Shaw*
Temporalities by *Russell West-Pavlov*
Travel Writing by *Carl Thompson*
The Unconscious by *Antony Easthope*

FAIRY TALE

Andrew Teverson

Routledge
Taylor & Francis Group

LONDON AND NEW YORK

First published 2013
by Routledge
2 Park Square, Milton Park, Abingdon, Oxon OX14 4RN

Simultaneously published in the USA and Canada
by Routledge
711 Third Avenue, New York, NY 10017

Routledge is an imprint of the Taylor & Francis Group, an informa business

British Library Cataloguing in Publication Data
A catalogue record for this book is available from the British Library

Library of Congress Cataloging in Publication Data
Teverson, Andrew.
Fairy tale / Andrew Teverson.
pages cm. – (The new critical idiom)
Includes bibliographical references and index.
1. Fairy tales–History and criticism. I. Title.
PN3437.T46 2013
398.2–dc23
2012046371

ISBN: 978-0-415-61605-8 (hbk)
ISBN: 978-0-415-61606-5 (pbk)
ISBN: 978-0-203-36610-3 (ebk)

Typeset in Garamond
by Taylor & Francis Books

MIX
Paper from
responsible sources
FSC
www.fsc.org   FSC® C013056

Printed and bound in Great Britain by
TJ International Ltd, Padstow, Cornwall

For Hilda Cochrane, my mother.

Think what you would have been now, if instead of being fed with Tales and old wives' fables in childhood, you had been crammed with geography and natural history!

(Charles Lamb to Samuel Taylor Coleridge, 1802)

CONTENTS

Series editor's preface   viii
Acknowledgements   ix

Introduction   1

1   Definitions   10

2   The emergence of a literary genre: Early Modern
    Italy to the French salon   38

3   The consolidation of a genre: the Brothers Grimm
    to Hans Christian Andersen   61

4   The emergence of fairy-tale theory: Plato to Propp   83

5   Psychoanalysis, history and ideology: twentieth- and
    twenty-first-century approaches to fairy tale   109

Conclusion   140

    Glossary   144
    Bibliography   152
    Index   160

SERIES EDITOR'S PREFACE

The New Critical Idiom is a series of introductory books which seeks to extend the lexicon of literary terms, in order to address the radical changes which have taken place in the study of literature during the last decades of the twentieth century. The aim is to provide clear, well-illustrated accounts of the full range of terminology currently in use, and to evolve histories of its changing usage.

The current state of the discipline of literary studies is one where there is considerable debate concerning basic questions of terminology. This involves, among other things, the boundaries which distinguish the literary from the non-literary; the position of literature within the larger sphere of culture; the relationship between literatures of different cultures; and questions concerning the relation of literary to other cultural forms within the context of interdisciplinary studies.

It is clear that the field of literary criticism and theory is a dynamic and heterogeneous one. The present need is for individual volumes on terms which combine clarity of exposition with an adventurousness of perspective and a breadth of application. Each volume will contain as part of its apparatus some indication of the direction in which the definition of particular terms is likely to move, as well as expanding the disciplinary boundaries within which some of these terms have been traditionally contained. This will involve some re-situation of terms within the larger field of cultural representation, and will introduce examples from the area of film and the modern media in addition to examples from a variety of literary texts.

ACKNOWLEDGEMENTS

My thanks to John Drakakis for commissioning this study, and for his insightful comments and generous scholarly support throughout. I'm also grateful to Ruth Moody, Paula Clarke, Emma Hudson and Polly Dodson for their diligent editorial work in preparing the manuscript for publication. I've benefited in numerous ways from the dynamic intellectual and educational environment at Kingston University, so thanks to my colleagues there, and to my students past and present. I'd especially like to thank David Rogers and Martin McQuillan for helping me to preserve some space for research, and Linda Corcoran for finding me time to write in a busy schedule. The best insights concerning fairy tales and folk narratives come from conversation. Particularly important have been my conversations with Gill Gregory, Tom Teverson, Grant Gordon, Amy Greenhough, Silvia Storti, Camilla Schroeder, Leigh Money, and the children of Class 1B (2010) of Hitherfield School who helped educate me about fairy tales at an early stage of this project. Toby: thanks for sending me fairy tales and sorry I didn't have space to do justice to them here, but they are germinating in a special file. Acknowledgement must also go to Anu Garg for the word 'plurisignification', and for all the other words that arrive in my inbox daily. Finally, special thanks to Simone for support that it is beyond my powers to quantify, and to Dominic and Tristan for listening to hundreds of stories in the name of research, for assistance with the bibliography and index, and for the invention of the Grothers Brimm and their deathless classic, 'The Dwarf and the Seven Snow Whites'.

ACKNOWLEDGMENTS

INTRODUCTION

So this is the truth of it. The World of Magic has taken many forms in different times and places, and it has had many different names. It has changed its location, its geography and its laws, as the history of the Real World has moved from age to age.

(Salman Rushdie, *Luka and the Fire of Life*, Rushdie 2010a: 139)

THREE GIRLS IN A WOOD

Consider the following three stories: in the first, a girl in a red cloak is sent through the woods by her mother to take her sick grandmother some provisions. On the way, she meets a wolf who asks her where she is going, and the girl, perhaps unwisely, tells him that she is going to Grandma's house. The wolf races to the grandmother's cottage and gets there before her. It devours the grandmother, and then, when the girl arrives, it devours her too. And that is the end of the story.

The next story is similar: a girl in a red cloak is sent through the woods by her mother to take her sick grandmother some provisions. On the way this girl also meets a wolf and, not having the benefits of the first girl's example, she too tells the wolf where she is going. The wolf races to Grandmother's cottage ahead of her and devours the grandmother. Then, when the girl arrives, she also is devoured. Fortunately, however, a huntsman has heard the commotion in the cottage, and appears in time to cut open the wolf's belly and rescue the girl and her grandmother. The wolf's belly is filled with stones and sewn up, and when it wakes and goes to the well to drink, it topples in and is drowned.

The third story is similar again, but once more there are differences: yet another girl is sent through the woods by her mother to take her sick grandmother some provisions. This girl does not have a red hood, but she is accosted by a wolf. Again, she tells the wolf where she is going, and again the wolf races ahead, gets to Grandmother's cottage first, and devours the grandmother; he also does some unpleasant things, like putting her blood in a jar and putting some of her flesh in the pantry. The girl arrives, and having drunk the blood and eaten the flesh of Granny, undresses for the wolf. But when she realises that the wolf is going to devour her, she plays a trick on him. She says she has to go outside to pee. The wolf ties a piece of string to her leg so she won't get away. But once the girl is outside, she ties the string to a tree and runs off. The wolf tugs the string to see if the girl is still there and, because it is tied to the tree, it thinks she is. This gives the girl the vital time she needs to escape, and in this manner she manages to get away.

Of course, this story will be familiar to readers; it is the story of 'Little Red Riding Hood'. But perhaps not all versions of this story are equally familiar. The second version, in which Little Red is rescued by a hunter, is probably the best-known version today because it is the version that is most commonly used as a basis for the retellings that appear in children's picture books. This is the version that was published in the first volume of the collection of 'household tales' made by the Brothers Grimm in Germany in the early nineteenth century, supplied for them by Marie Hassenpflug who lived near them in Kassel. Prior to the publication of the Grimms' collection, however, there was another version of the story in circulation (the first version above), which had been written down in 1697 by the French court official, Charles Perrault, ostensibly from the narration of his son's nurse. This version of the tale, with its bleak ending, has become less common as readers of fairy tales, or at least their parents, have come to favour the comforting and romantic, over the punitive and the cautionary ('Control your impulses or else!' Perrault's story warns). Nevertheless, Perrault's narrative remains commonly anthologised, and sometimes still appears in books aimed at children. The third version of the story summarised above, with its trickster heroine who outwits the wolf, is probably the least familiar today, though it might be argued that it is this trickster **folk tale**, more than any other version, that, in spirit, inhabits modern revisitations of the 'Little Red Riding Hood' narrative such as Roald Dahl's poem 'Little Red Riding Hood and the Wolf' (1982), David Slade's film *Hard Candy* (2005) and Danielle Wood's story 'Rosie Little in the Mother Country' (Wood 2008), all of which, like the tale of the French tricksteress, emphasise the capacity of the smart heroine to outwit the predatory wolf figure. This particular version of the story was told by François and Louis Briffault to the folklorist Achille Millien in Nièvre, France, in about 1885, and published, from Millien's manuscript recording, by Paul Delarue in the anthology *The Borzoi Book of French Folk Tales* in 1956. It is probable, however, that the story is much older than Millien's 1885 recording. Indeed, it may be the case that it predates the literary version that Perrault wrote down some two hundred years earlier. Delarue (1989: 16–20), Alan Dundes (1989: 13–14), Maria Tatar (1999: 3–4), Jack Zipes (2001: 744–45), Robert Darnton (2001: 9–12) and Catherine Orenstein (2002: 71) have each accepted this argument, postulating that Perrault appropriated an 'original' folk tale from oral tradition and 'dramatically revised' it, adding in details that are not present in the folk tradition, such as the red hood, and removing others, such as the happy ending which is found in most oral variations on the story except those directly based upon Perrault (Orenstein 2002: 71).

Ultimately, of course, there is no direct evidence for this speculation: Perrault did not keep any records, and before the nineteenth century oral folk tales left few reliable traces. Widespread evidence of cognate oral versions of the story in different parts of the world, however, many of which share story elements that are not to be found in Perrault's version, suggest on balance that it is highly likely that this story existed in oral tradition before 1697 in forms comparable with the Briffault narration, and that Perrault adapted the story considerably for his own ends (Delarue 1989: 18–19).

The three versions of 'Little Red Riding Hood' cited above, combined with the many hundred more that have been collected over the last two centuries, illustrate the particular challenges and rewards of studying fairy tales from a scholarly point of view. First of all: fairy tales do not have single, stable originals that we can depend upon as source texts; they proliferate as narratives, and it is often unclear which version, if any, should have priority over others. It is usually possible to identify a 'first recorded' literary version of a particular narrative type (in this case, Perrault's), but this version is not necessarily the most accurate representation of the story as it exists in tradition, and it may be the case that there are stories collected at a later date (in this case, Millien's) that are thought to reflect tradition with greater accuracy. To add to this difficulty, it is probable that the texts available, both oral and literary, will differ significantly from one another in plotting, in style, in intended audience, and in social function. Perrault's story is designed to appeal to the tastes and preconceptions of the courtly society of late-seventeenth-century France; the Grimms' story has been adapted to suit the requirements of the early nineteenth-century middle-class household; and the Millien narrative must be understood in relation to at least two contexts: the situation in which it was collected, in nineteenth-century France, but also the possible historical situations from which it is presumed to derive: the world of the French peasant in the seventeenth and eighteenth century (Darnton 2001: 16–18). When we ask what a narrative like 'Little Red Riding Hood' means, therefore, we also have to ask ourselves which 'Little Red Riding Hood' we are speaking about, for in each case, the story emerges in a different context, with different features and a different set of potential significances.

This leads us to the second major challenge involved in the study of fairy tale: that any one narrative, because it is not owned by a single author, or produced in any one time or culture, must also be understood as being culturally and historically layered within itself. As a generic form, the fairy tale is a many-tongued genre, a cultural palimpsest; because even as it speaks of the time in which it is told, it carries the memory of the other times in which it has circulated and flourished. It bears the print of the hand that holds it, but under that print it carries the marks of earlier hands. Thus as we read the stories of Perrault, we see in these stories the lineaments of older, Italian storytellers; as we enter German forests with the Brothers Grimm, we are able to glimpse the lines of human transit that tie nineteenth-century Germany to eleventh-century India; and as we read the polished literary adaptations of Victorian Englishmen, we hear, or think we hear, an echo of feudal roots. The fairy tale may, as a result, seem timeless, but it seems timeless not because it has no history, but because it has too many histories, because it is plural and many voiced. The scholar of fairy tales has to be sensitive to this multiplicity of voices; to seek to understand the story under analysis as both a unique story, the product of a specific time and place, and as a story that has circulated in numerous different contexts and taken numerous different forms.

A third challenge involved in the study of fairy tale concerns the extent of the interpretative models available to the scholar. Fairy tales, because they speak in an apparently symbolic language, because they are thought to be ancient, because they are iconic, because they are communal, because they are part of our collective consciousness, invite interpretation. This phenomenon is embodied in the familiar question posed of fairy tales: What does it really mean? What are the true significances of 'Little Red Riding Hood'? In two hundred years of folk narrative analysis, a wealth of solutions has been offered to this problem. The solar mythologists of the nineteenth century regarded fairy tales as the degenerate remains of ancient cosmic mythologies, and interpreted them as narratives about the sun's journey through the heavens. Anthropological folklorists of the same era rejected the idea that fairy tales originate in the coherent mythological systems of antique civilisations, and argued instead that they are **survivals** of savage practices that codify the rites and rituals of our primitive ancestors. More recently, scholars of the psychoanalytical school have argued that fairy tales are disguised manifestations of latent fears

and desires that well up from our innermost selves; whilst scholars who favour a more historical approach have argued that fairy
tales supply us with information about the material concerns of
particular societies at particular times. And this does not exhaust
the possibilities of interpretation: feminist critics have argued that
canonical fairy tales operate as mechanisms designed to foster the
patriarchal control of women by promoting to young and impressionable readers the idea that women are either passive and good
or active and evil; Marxist critics, likewise, have suggested that
fairy tales, in their authorised forms, are potent carriers of ideological
instruction that shape nascent identities in ways that are most
beneficial to those with power in society. Little Red Riding
Hood, in this bristling forest of interpretation, takes on diverse
disguises: she is the flaming red sun in transit through the day,
devoured by the wolf/night at evening; she is a savage maiden, in
communion with the animistic powers of nature, enduring a rite
of passage from innocence to experience; she is a codification of
primitive laws, on the cusp of transgressing an antique rule of
forest etiquette; she is a vehicle for moral ideas, reminding young
girls to listen to their mothers and shun strange men; she is a life-line
thrown to forest-dwelling peasants who, without her example,
might wander from the path and become prey to *real* wolves; she
is a flourishing adolescent, experimental and curious, testing out
her newly discovered sexual powers; she is an allegory of vulnerable but resurgent German innocence, preyed upon by vicious
French invaders; she is a folk-trickster, given the licence of the
plucky underdog to outwit the adversarial forces of bleak reality
arrayed against her; and she is a vehicle for the oppression of
women by men, a helpless victim, who is punished with rape
because she does not heed the censures of male authority (in Dundes
1989, see P. Saintyves: 71–88; Hans-Wolf Jäger: 89–120; Jack
Zipes: 121–28; Bruno Bettelheim: 168–91; see also Zipes 1993:
17–37 and Tatar 1999: 3–10).

This kaleidoscope of interpretations tells us several things
about the fairy tale: it tells us that the fairy tale has the quality of
plurisignification: that it is rich in potential meanings, and can
take on diverse significances depending on how it is being used
and by whom. But it also tells us that the fairy tale is vulnerable

to scholarly exploitation: that it is a form of writing that, because it appears to have symbolic significance, is relatively easy to press into the service of each new scholarly vogue. As Lutz Röhrich cautions, 'the astounding number and variety of answers' to the problem of what such narratives mean 'raises considerable doubts about ... method': it implies that interpreters are bringing 'more to the folktale than they get out of it'; that folk-tale interpretation is being guided by 'preconceived views developed [from] outside ... rather than [by] the texts themselves' (Röhrich 1991: 6–7). As an antidote to this, Röhrich proposes the following principle: that '[i]nterpretations must ... proceed deductively from the material if they are to do the folktale justice as an item of folk poetry' (7). This is not to say that the methodologies of analysis that have been applied to the fairy tale are necessarily misleading: fairy tales do have latent content that reflects specific cultural anxieties and desires; they do seek to impose social and cultural codes upon their audiences; and they are often used as allegories of natural phenomena or political events. But no one of these methods of interpretation can be applied unilaterally and without reference to the specific set of narratives under investigation: the unconscious of the fairy tale will shift and change with different societal pressures; the political functions of the fairy tale will be remade afresh by each new storyteller; and the story that is used to oppress and marginalise in one era can be used to liberate and protest in another. Thus the fairy tale becomes a gauge of shifting human interests and shifting social mores: a receptacle of cultural preoccupations that is forever being reinvented.

The quotation taken from Salman Rushdie's novel *Luka and the Fire of Life* (Rushdie 2010a) in the epigraph for this chapter is an eloquent expression of this idea: fairy tales, like myths and legends, take different forms at different times, and the forms they take reflect the places in which they have settled, and the particular historical moments in which they have been recorded, interpreted and preserved. Fairy tale is not universal or timeless; neither is it innocent of history and politics. On the contrary, it speaks powerfully of the times in which it has been told.

These principles give critical direction to the present study which seeks, throughout, to place the development of fairy tale, and the emergence of fairy-tale criticism, in social and historical perspective. Chapter 1 seeks to define the fairy tale by presenting it as a metamorphic genre, shaped and reshaped by shifting attitudes to the concept of the 'folk'. Chapter 2 traces the emergence of the fairy tale as a recognisable literary form, briefly surveying the manifestation of fairy-tale plots in ancient literatures, but focusing primarily upon the innovations in fairy-tale writing made in Early Modern Italy and Enlightenment France by the writers Giovan Francesco Straparola (c. 1480–c. 1558), Giambattista Basile (c. 1575–1632), Marie-Catherine d'Aulnoy (c. 1650–1705) and Charles Perrault (1628–1703). Chapter 3 extends this historical account, concentrating upon consolidation of the modern European model of the literary fairy tale in the work of the Brothers Grimm (Jacob, 1785–1863, Wilhelm, 1786–1859) and Hans Christian Andersen (1805–75). In the fourth and fifth chapters, this study then shifts focus to concentrate upon critical and theoretical responses to the genre. Chapter 4 examines shifting attitudes to the popular traditional tale from the classical period to the mid-twentieth century, looking in particular at the efforts made by scholars in the nineteenth and early twentieth century to understand where fairy tales came from, how they were disseminated across time and space, how they can be catalogued and classified, and what formal properties they have. Chapter 5, following on from this, investigates twentieth- and twenty-first-century endeavours to understand the meaning of fairy tales, concentrating upon psychoanalytic, Marxist and socio-historical analyses of the genre. This chapter also brings us to the fairy tale's present, showing how the influence of critical and conceptual analysis of fairy tales, in particular feminist analysis, has helped shape recent revisionist approaches to fairy tale in literature and film. These revisionist approaches, it is argued, engage in a complex intertextual response to fairy tale, seeking simultaneously to recuperate some aspects of tradition and critique others.

Throughout, the fairy tale is understood as a form about which it is difficult to generalise: it is a genre that has been shaped by the East and the West, the North and the South; it has existed in visual culture, literary culture, and oral tradition; and at any one time it is capable of expressing an admixture of dominant, residual and emergent ideas. This quality gives the contemporary response to fairy tales one of its distinctive features: it allows writers, filmmakers and artists to play one model of fairy tale off against another (Warner 1994: 4). But though contemporary approaches to fairy tale have tended to self-consciously foreground the process by which one story replies to another, the fairy tale has, in an important sense, always been dialogical, since new fairy tales in every period necessarily respond, in manifold ways, to existing tradition. The present study aims to capture something of the character of this engagement with tradition, and in so doing to show how the fairy tale reflects the complex processes of exchange and transmission that form the basis of human culture.

1

DEFINITIONS

Pops, music is music. All music is folk music. I ain't never heard no horse sing a song.

(Louis Armstrong, quoted in Krebs 1971: np)

WHO THE FOLK ARE YOU?

Because the fairy tale is widely believed to have emerged, at some point in its long, complex and often untraceable history, from the mass of fictional forms invented, enjoyed and disseminated by the 'folk', it is generally classified as a sub-genre of folk narrative. But this begs a question: who are the folk? And what kinds of narrative did they produce? If we apply Louis Armstrong's prescription for 'folk music' to 'folk narrative' the category disappears: all narratives are 'folk' narratives, because all narratives are necessarily the product of some human agency. As book publishers and music producers know, however, the prefix 'folk' has a very particular, and often highly marketable, set of cultural resonances. It suggests something that is of the people, and therefore close to the roots of culture; it suggests a mode of expression that is sincere, popular and 'true to itself'; and it implies a form of art that is unaffected and unselfconscious. This set of associations may be traced back to the closing decades of the eighteenth century, when a group of German writers and intellectuals, seeking to root an embattled German identity in a long and respectable past, invented the concept of a pure and unaffected *volk*, who might act as guardians of an ancient national tradition. This *volk* were imagined to be illiterate and lower class, but nevertheless eloquent and expressive; they were, invariably, stationed in the countryside, indelibly bound to the rhythms of the seasons and the bucolic pace of the natural world, and they perpetuated a tradition which had, in its essence, remained unchanged since ancient times. As Wilhelm Grimm writes in the preface to the first volume of the *Kinder- und Hausmärchen* [Children's and Household Tales], in which these ideas are expressed most influentially, 'the riches of German poetry from olden times' have been 'kept alive' in 'folk songs and ... innocent household tales,' because these stories represent the untrammelled imagination ... not yet warped by the perversities of life (Tatar 2003: 252–53).

So potent has this myth of the folk been that it survives today in the common assumption that the transmitters of 'folk' narrative are the common people, that the materials these people transmit are inestimably ancient, and that these materials, because of the illiteracy of their carriers, were orally disseminated in the first instance. In J. A. Cuddon's *Dictionary of Literary Terms and Literary Theory* (third edition, 1992), for instance, 'folk literature' is described as being 'for the most part ... the creation of primitive and illiterate people' and as belonging 'to oral tradition' (Cuddon 1992: 346). Even in the nineteenth century, however, scholars were beginning to mistrust this description. In 1893, for instance, the Australian-born Jewish folklorist Joseph Jacobs, in an essay that was ahead of its time in many respects, asked who the 'folk' might be, and came up with an answer that was quite different from the one given by many of his contemporaries. The 'folk' that mediate **'folklore'**, he argued, if there is such a thing as a 'folk' at all, do not represent a single demographic group, and do not come from a specific geographical area. Folklore is produced by all classes, rich and poor, educated and uneducated, and it is produced in all regions, urban and rural. It also travels across national borders when the people that carry it travel over them, making it into an international and transitive form of culture, rather than a testament to a sheltered, ethnically pure, national tradition. 'The folk', as Jacobs writes, 'is many-headed … and often many-minded', and 'when we come to realise what we mean by saying a custom, a tale, a myth arose from the Folk … we must come to the conclusion that the said Folk is a fraud, a delusion, a myth' (Jacobs 1893: 233–34). If it is to exist at all, Jacobs goes on, it can only exist under the assumption that everybody is part of the folk, and that when we attribute a cultural product to the folk we are simply giving a name to our ignorance, stating that 'we do not know to whom a proverb, a tale, a custom, a myth owes its origin' so we are going to say 'it originated among the Folk' (236). This folklore, to which we all contribute, moreover, can also, Jacobs insists, be found in all periods of human history. It is not a thing of the past, characterised by beliefs and rituals that are necessarily obsolete and anachronistic, but is often contemporary with human society. 'Survivals are folk-lore,' Jacobs avers, 'but folk-lore need not be all survivals':

> We ought to learn valuable hints as to the spread of folk-lore by studying the Folk of to-day. The music-hall, from this point of view, will have its charm for the folk-lorist, who will there find the *Volkslieder* of to-day. The spread of popular sayings, even the rise of new words, provided they be folk-words, should be regarded as a part of the study of folk-lore.
>
> (Jacobs 1893: 237)

Recent analysis of folk narratives has increasingly endorsed Jacobs's arguments. Folk narratives, it is generally agreed by folklorists, are stories which have survived for significant periods of time in popular tradition by being passed on, from storyteller to storyteller, both spatially across cultures and communities, and temporally from generation to generation. They do not, however, need to have loomed up from distant antiquity in order to be classified as such, neither do they need to have been exclusively, or even originally, oral narratives in their modes of transmission.

The story 'King of the Cats' (ML6070b),[1] for example, which is usually classified as a folk tale or a migratory legend, and which has been collected as an oral fiction in several different nations at several different periods, is first found as an episode in William Baldwin's proto-novel *Beware the Cat*, written in 1553. Baldwin's story, narrated in the fiction by a servant, concerns a man who, while riding through Kankwood 'about certain business' is confronted by a cat who leaps out of a bush and speaks to him 'plainly twice or thrice' the words 'Commend me unto Titton Tatton and to Puss thy Catton, and tell her that Grimalkin is dead' (Baldwin 1988: 11). The man, having heard this strange feline communication, continues about his business, and on returning home he tells his wife the full story and repeats the talking cat's words, upon which his own cat, who has 'hearkened unto the tale', looks upon him sadly and says 'And is Grimalkin dead? Then farewell dame' (11).

This same narrative has subsequently been recorded in diverse contexts with diverse variations. A version of the story has been collected from County Durham featuring a farmer from Staindrop named Johnny Reed who is told that 'Mally Dixen's deed' (Philip 1992: 346). There is also a Shropshire tale, featuring the death of 'old Peter', news of which causes a family cat to disappear up a chimney shrieking 'By Jove! Old Peter's dead! And I'm King o' the cats!' (Philip 1992: 346). Such variation and repetition is characteristic of migratory traditions, and attests to the fact that the story has survived in popular tradition for four hundred years, altering subtly in its details as it has passed from teller to teller and writer to writer. The fact of the story's broad dissemination since Baldwin's first inscription of it, however, does not necessarily guarantee an oral origin. It is certainly possible that Baldwin, in 1553, took it from a flourishing popular, oral tradition, which may in turn explain why he gives the narration to a servant; but equally it is possible, as the recent editors of *Beware the Cat* argue, that Baldwin invented the story as part of a work of literature (Baldwin 1988: 60 n. 11.9).

A similar genealogy might be given for the well-known tale 'Jack and the Beanstalk' (ATU328 'The Boy Steals the Giant's Treasure').[2] This narrative has been found in oral traditions throughout the world, and is particularly common along the lines of communication established by British exploration and British settlement from the sixteenth century onwards. Oral versions of it have been collected in Mandeville, Jamaica, for example, where it was told to the American folklorist Martha Warren Beckwith by a 19-year-old man named Clarence Tathum in 1919 or 1921 (Beckwith 1924: 150), and in the Appalachian Mountains in the American South, as recorded by Richard Chase in his collection *The Jack Tales* (1943). Joseph Jacobs has also claimed that the version of 'Jack and the Beanstalk' that he included in his *English Fairy Tales* of 1890, and that has subsequently become the basis of most modern retellings, was told to him by his nurse in Australia when he was six years old (Jacobs 1890: n. 13). Before any of these oral traditions had been collected, however, 'Jack and the Beanstalk' enjoyed popularity as a chapbook narrative in early-nineteenth-century Britain, having been published as *The History of Mother Twaddle, and the Marvellous Atchievements of Her Son Jack* by 'B.A. T.' in 1807 and as *The History of Jack and the Bean-Stalk* by Benjamin Tabart in 1809. The oldest reliable allusion to the story, moreover, comes in a literary skit, 'Enchantment Demonstrated in the Story of Jack Spriggins and the Enchanted Bean', which appeared in the second edition of *Round About Our Coal-Fire: Or Christmas Entertainments* published in 1734. On the assumption that 'parody implies popularity', this skit, no doubt, indicates the existence of earlier mediations of the story (Philip 1992: 9). There is certainly evidence that the rhyme 'Fe Fi Fo Fum', associated with the tale, existed in association with another story, the story of Childe Rowland, as early as Shakespeare's *King Lear* (1605; see Jacobs 1891), and some scholars trace **motifs** to be found in the story to depictions of giant plants and acts of giant-slaying in Norse mythology and ancient Indian traditions (see Opie and Opie 1980: 213; and Goldberg 2001). But the story in its current form, as it appears in children's books, pantomimes, and films, can only be reliably dated to the early eighteenth century and to its appearance as a popular, mass-market *literary* production.

Both these examples, 'King of the Cats' and 'Jack and the Beanstalk', share the following characteristics: they are (a) popular stories that are or have been widely known and enjoyed by all classes of society, (b) stories that have survived in multiple versions, at different times, and in different regions, and have therefore, in the course of time, even if not originally, become communal property, (c) tales that are (as a result of (b)) not associated exclusively with the authorship of any one individual, (d) stories that have circulated freely between oral, literary and other media, and (e) stories that, according to Georges and Jones, 'we judge traditional ... because they are based on known precedents or models, and ... because they serve as evidence of continuities and consistencies through time and space in human knowledge, thought, belief and feeling' (Georges and Jones 1995: 1). What these stories do not give evidence of, however, is the tenacious Romantic belief that fictions of this sort are necessarily oral in origin, antique in age, or peasant in extraction. When defining the fairy tale as a form of folk narrative, therefore, we should be suspicious of obstinate Romantic conceptions of the fairy tale. This does not mean, however, *pace* Armstrong, that the category must disappear altogether. Folk narrative remains an institutionally recognisable form; and it also remains a form with some distinctive and enduring generic features.

THE TYPES OF THE FOLK NARRATIVE

The broad category of folk narrative is generally subdivided into three principal forms by scholars: the myth, the legend and the folk tale. This tripartite division has formed the basis of most taxonomies of folk narrative since Wilhelm and Jacob Grimm devoted major works to each category: the *Kinder- und Hausmärchen* (1812–15), *Deutsche Sagen* [German Legends] (1816–18) and *Deutsche Mythologie* [German Myths] (1835). The boundaries between all these categories are fluid, and distinctions cannot be imposed inflexibly on what is, in reality, a rich and metamorphic body of popular materials; nevertheless, as a convenient rule of thumb, it is possible to make some useful basic distinctions between them as follows.

The legend is a story that has become attached, at some point in time, to a specified historical personage, a specified locality, or a specified event. It is also a fiction that requires an agreement between storyteller and audience that they will both, for the purposes of the story, regard the events described as having taken place. Legends include apocryphal stories about well-known historical personages (King Arthur, Sir Walter Raleigh, Vlad the Impaler, Dick Whittington), semi-factual narrative cycles concerning cultural, or more properly, sub-cultural, heroes (Robin Hood, Nanny of the Maroons, Phoolan Devi), and stories that concern particular localities (The Lambton Worm, The Giant of Dalston Mill). Myths, like legends, also make claims to recount true events, though unlike legends they do not take place in recorded historical time, but 'in a world supposed to have preceded the present order' (Thompson 1977: 9). They characteristically deal with 'grand' subjects such as heroes, gods or the universe, and they tend, as a result, to fulfil culturally important functions for a specific community or nation: establishing a narrative of foundation for the community, idealising its values by embodying them in a specific hero or group of heroes, and codifying aspects of its belief system. This definition of myth was established most influentially by the anthropologist Bronislaw Malinowski in his collection of essays *Myth in Primitive Psychology* (1926) that focused on the mythologies of the Trobriand Islanders. Myth, Malinowski argued, 'expresses, enhances, and codifies belief' and in so doing it fulfils its main cultural function, which is 'to strengthen tradition and endow it with a greater value and prestige by tracing it back to a higher, better, more supernatural reality of initial events' (Malinowski 1926: 23 and 125). It is this sacred function of myths, according to the folklorist William Bascom, that enables us to distinguish myths most effectively from other forms of folk narrative. Legends, Bascom proposed, are narratives that are, at the source of their telling, 'believed to be true and to contain important factual information'; myths, in their original cultural contexts, are 'regarded as not merely true, but as venerable and sacred'; and folk tales are narratives that, in contrast to legends and myths, are regarded as purely fictional both by their tellers and their hearers (Bascom 1981: 44 and 97–98). This formulation, as Bascom points out, would allow for the possibility of transit between these genres: a myth or legend that is no longer believed to have truth-value may, in the course of time, become a folk tale; and a narrative that is, in one society, regarded as a folk tale may, in another society, be regarded as a myth (Bascom 1981: 102).

If myths deal with grand subjects (both formally and conceptually), folk tales are more quotidian in their concerns. The protagonists of myth are distant figures, incomparably greater than ordinary men and women, and the objective of the narratives in which their adventures appear is to make readers or hearers realise that they could not be like the personages depicted, or achieve the feats that are within their grasp. The protagonists of folk tales, by contrast, even when they are princes and princesses, seem 'more like us', and more concerned with the common human desire to make a living, eat well, marry someone pleasant or successful, and steer clear of danger. Like myths, of course, folk tales are interested in heroism, but where myths celebrate the heroism of those who are first in a society, the 'likely' heroes, folk tales tend to favour the unlikely heroes: the plucky peasant, the youngest son, the neglected daughter and the thumb-sized boy. Folk tales are, therefore, in the nautical terminology applied to folk narrative by the Danish folklorist Axel Olrik, *achtergewicht* (stern weighted) rather than *toppgewicht* (bow weighted) (Dundes 1999: 93). Moreover, whilst myths tend to engage with grand explanations and theological structures, folk tales tend to ignore the cosmos and divinity and focus instead upon hearth rug and humanity. For all the palaces that appear in folk tales, they are, as the title of the Grimm collection has it, *hausmärchen* (household tales). They take place in the familiar settings of town and countryside, and they depict their protagonists triumphing over common adversity such as poverty or hunger, through some clever ruse or some extraordinary stroke of luck, or, if the protagonist is not sufficiently quick witted or sufficiently lucky, suffering amusing calamities because of their idiocy. Representative European folk tales would include the story of 'The Fisherman and his Wife' (ATU555), written in Pomeranian dialect by Philipp Otto Runge and passed to the Brothers Grimm for inclusion in the first volume of their tales in 1812. In this story a fisherman, having caught a talking fish, is persuaded by his wife to ask the fish for greater and greater rewards until he asks for the unaskable (for his wife to be God), at which point he and his wife are returned to the poverty-stricken state in which they started out. This story may be considered to be a folk tale because it has ordinary protagonists (a fisherman and his wife), dwells on everyday activities (fishing), and, to begin with at least, has a familiar setting (the cottage). It includes magical events, as folk tales often do, but it remains rooted in a familiar world, and its magic makes possible the fulfilment of readily understandable wishes: wealth, a nice house and material satisfaction.

Another representative example of a folk tale is the story of 'Clever Jack' related to Henry Mayhew by a 16-year-old vagrant in a London workhouse in the 1860s and recorded in his *London Labour and the London Poor* (Mayhew 1864, vol. III: 388–90). In this story a series of narratives is told about the ruses of Clever Jack including one in which Jack, pretending to be an angel who has come to take a parson to heaven, persuades the parson to put himself in one sack and all his gold plate into another. Jack promptly takes the parson to a gentleman who gives him a horsewhipping, and he keeps the bag full of gold plate and money for himself. Mayhew's informant, an 'intelligent-looking boy' in 'a series of ragged coats', described the story as 'one ... that I invented till I learnt it' (Philip 1992: 19), but in fact the story is an international tale type (AT1525, 'The Master Thief') and is at least as old as Giovan Francesco Straparola's Venetian collection *Le piacevoli notti* (*The Pleasant Nights*), published in the mid-sixteenth century, where it first appeared in Europe in print.

The dominant mode of such stories, it will be apparent, is comic: we either laugh at the antics of the foolish protagonists and take pleasure in the elaborate forms of their suffering, or we applaud the cunning ruses of the trickster hero and revel good humouredly in his or her high-spirited refusal to be subjected to the authority of those with greater power or greater physical might. These stories, of course, may also have moral functions: 'The Fisherman and his Wife' warns readers and hearers not to press their ambitions too far lest they be punished for their greed and presumption. These moral functions may also reflect particular social outlooks. A Marxist reading of 'The Fisherman and his Wife' might see the narrative as a bourgeois fiction that warns the peasantry against overbold endeavours to escape their allotted class; equally, a feminist reading of the story might seek to expose its coded patriarchal messages: that men ought not to be led by the desires of their wives, that women's desires are often irrational and extreme, and that a woman with power is dangerous.

The folk tale, however, is not fundamentally a moral form, even though many of its collectors have struggled to make it fulfil moral purposes. The cardinal rule for folk-tale heroes is not to be good but to be clever. Hence, those folk protagonists who exercise cunning, and approach the world in a spirit of witty irreverence, tend to do well, even if they are, like Clever Jack, cheats, thieves and liars. Those protagonists who exhibit failings of wit, by contrast, tend to fare badly, even if they do not do anything that might be considered morally reprehensible.

As this comic dimension might suggest, the dominant function of the folk tale is entertainment. Whilst the myth functions to codify belief, the folk tale functions to distract, to enchant, to help pass some time and smooth the passage of days. In part, this identifies the folk tale as a medium appropriate for times of relaxation or leisure. In some contexts, however, this form of narration has also been used to facilitate work, particularly work of a manual and repetitive character. A prominent working context in which folk tales were told, as Maria Tatar (2003: 112–13) and Marina Warner (1995: 22–23) have observed, was the spinning room, 'where spinning yarn helped to while away the hours devoted to spinning flax' (Tatar 2003: 112–13). It is often possible, in folk tales and fairy tales, to see the traces of these occupational contexts. For example, several of the Grimms' tales feature spinners or acts of spinning, and offer the consolatory promise that such rigours can be alleviated or escaped. The story of 'Rumpelstiltskin' (ATU500 'The Name of the Helper') represents the fantasy that a life of drudgery in the spinning room might be miraculously replaced with life as a pampered queen, as does the related story of 'The Three Spinners' (ATU501). In the latter tale, a 'lazy maiden', after a foolish boast on the part of her mother, is taken, by a queen, to her castle and told that if she is able to spin an improbable amount of flax she will be allowed to marry the queen's son. Initially the attainment of this goal seems unlikely, since the maiden does not have the spinning skills her mother has claimed for her. The maiden, however, receives unexpected assistance from three old women, the first of whom has a broad flat foot, the second a large lower lip that hangs over her chin, and the third an immense thumb, deformities that are the products of a long spinning career: the flat foot comes from treading the spinning wheel, the drooping lip from licking the flax, and the immense thumb from twisting the thread. In return for their help these women ask only to be invited to the maiden's wedding to the prince, a promise which is duly fulfilled, and which prepares the ground for the comic denouement of the tale; for when the prince sees these women and hears how they have come by their deformities, he immediately commands that his beautiful wife shall '[n]ever ever ... touch a spinning wheel again'. 'Thus,' the tale concludes, 'she was able to rid herself of the terrible task of spinning flax' (Grimm and Grimm 1992: 57). We may imagine that this story developed as a narrative in spinning circles, and that it had the additional function of commenting upon the life and lot of the spinner. On the one hand, it recognises the unhappy working life of the spinner, and so gives some measure of recognition and consolation for sufferings endured; on the other hand it is a wish-fulfilment that allows teller and hearers to fantasise about the marvellous possibility of being relieved from the arduous burden of spinning forever.

TYPES OF THE FOLK TALE

The narrative form described above is, arguably, the classic form of the folk tale: the short, earthy, tragic-comic tale of working life. For many readers, collectors and commentators there are no clear differences between these kinds of folk tale and the fairy tale: one blends into another like the colours on a Rothko canvas. This ambiguity is, to some extent, evidenced by the fact that one would not have to look far to find the stories of 'The Fisherman and his Wife', 'The Three Spinners' or 'Clever Jack' described as 'fairy tales' or inserted into 'fairy tale' collections. Theorists of folk narrative, however, have proposed further divisions within the category of 'folk tale' in order to define the objects of folk-narrative analysis and folk-narrative collection more precisely. In Antti Aarne and Stith Thompson's *The Types of the Folktale* (1928), folk tales are divided into Animal Tales, Ordinary Folk-Tales, Jokes

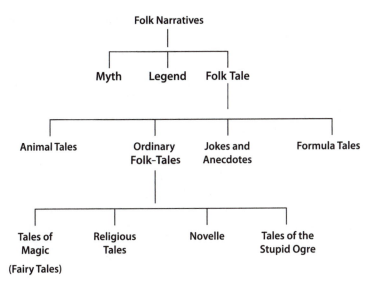

Figure 1.1

and Anecdotes, and Formula Tales. The category of Ordinary Folk-Tales is then further subdivided into Tales of Magic, Religious Tales, Novelle (Romantic Tales), and Tales of the Stupid Ogre. The genealogy of the fairy tale, based on this classification system would look something like Figure 1.1.

Katherine M. Briggs, in her *Dictionary of British Folk-Tales in the English Language* (Briggs 1970–71), offers a slightly different organisation. In classifying British traditions, Briggs distinguishes between Folk Narratives and Folk Legends; she does not, however, find sufficient warrant for a category of British Myths. Folk Narratives are subdivided into Fables and Exempla, Fairy Tales, Jocular Tales, Novelle, and Nursery Tales. Folk Legends are subdivided according to the various entities with which British Legends habitually have dealings; for example Tales of Fairies, Tales of Giants, Tales of Black Dogs.

In the classic collections of folk tales, these various forms are jumbled up more or less indiscriminately. The Grimm collection includes a hotch-potch of 'etiologies, fables, animal tales, moralistic stories, jests, exempla, religious and other legends, and various mixed forms such as humorous religious tales and humorous magic tales' (Uther 2004: 9). Likewise, Joseph Jacobs's *English Fairy Tales* (Jacobs 1890), despite the specificity of his title, places, alongside 'classic' British fairy tales such as 'Tom Tit Tot' and 'The Rose Tree', a ragged host of nursery tales ('The Story of the Three Little Pigs'), cumulative tales ('Henny Penny'), 'prosed' ballads ('Binnorie'), picaresque chapbook narratives ('Jack the Giant Killer'), numbskull tales ('Mr Vinegar'), legends ('Whittington and his Cat'), **cautionary tales** ('Mr Miacca'), and tales of the fairies ('Kate Crackernuts' and 'Fairy Ointment'). Jacobs also smuggles into his collection of 'English' tales stories from Ireland, Scotland, Australia and North America. This jumbling of forms is part of what makes such collections intriguing, and neither authors nor readers are any worse for it. As Stith Thompson, in his wisdom, avers: scholars should avoid 'too subtle analysis' of folk-tale categories, firstly because their forms are 'not so rigid as the theoretician might wish,' and secondly, because the men and women who tell and record folk tales 'neither know nor care about [scholarly] distinctions' (Thompson 1977: 7 and 10). For the purposes of generic identification, however, it is useful to tease out some finer distinctions between forms of folk narrative, and in so doing to place the fairy tale in clearer relation to its brothers, sisters and cousins.

ANIMAL TALES AND FABLES

Animal tales are folk narratives that use anthropomorphised beasts as their primary characters. These tales generally give specific animals compartmentalised human character traits such as the *lazy* bear, the *cunning* fox or the *foolish* rabbit, and are therefore comparable to the visual and literary traditions of the Bestiary, which also use animal symbolism to comment meaningfully on human behaviour. Animal tales appear in the folk literature of all cultures, and can take various forms. The *Anansi* (spider man) stories from West Africa and the Caribbean, the Tortoise (*Ajapa*) stories of the Yoruba, and the tales of Brer Rabbit in African-American tradition are trickster narratives in which a cunning animal tricks or otherwise takes advantage of less mentally adroit beasts; the narrative types used as inspiration for Rudyard Kipling's *Just So* stories (1902) are explanatory tales (alternatively, etiological tales or pourquoi tales) that frame a fictive, and often fanciful, justification for the particular physical features of an animal ('How the Leopard Got His Spots'); and the Ancient Greek stories associated with the name of Aesop, or the narratives gathered in the classical Indian compendium the *Panchatantra* between the third and fifth century, are fables in which the actions of the animal characters are used to make a moral point or to illustrate canny political or social behaviour.

Animal tales can often be confused with fairy tales, and frequently appear alongside fairy tales in compendia of popular narratives. Unlike animal tales, however, fairy tales tend to focus upon human protagonists in the first instance, and only include animals in secondary roles, as helpers or as opponents ('Puss in Boots'). Even in tales where an animal is a central character because a human protagonist has been magically translated into animal form, as in 'Beauty and the Beast' narratives, the important factor is the animal's inward humanity, and the capacity for the beast to be humanised. Fairy tales, one might conclude, are fundamentally about humanity, and one of their central functions is to dramatise the human condition.

RELIGIOUS TALES

Religious tales are fictions which address sacred subjects or sacred themes. They are stories that exist in popular culture, and that, unlike the stories that appear in authorised religious texts, are apocryphal and unofficial. Such stories often communicate superstitious ideas that would not be endorsed in more orthodox forms of the religion. Most collections of fairy tales include some religious elements; for instance, the Brothers Grimm rewrote the stories in their collection successively over nearly half a century to increase the Christian content of these fictions. Many classic fairy tales also include religious figures as prominent characters (the Virgin Mary, the Devil), although religious references alone do not suffice to make a religious tale. A religious tale must have a consistent theological focus, an instructional intention, and one or more characters derived from a religious tradition; they can also take the form of a parable or allegory, in which the entertaining popular fiction is used to illustrate a moral or religious principle. Fairy tales, or elements of fairy tales, may be used as parables, or they may be given allegorical dimensions by specific storytellers and writers. Most fairy tales, however, do not develop as religious tales, parables or allegories in the first instance, since fairy tales are, in the main, fictions designed to entertain that do not resort to programmatic secondary-level meaning systems, or to overt dogmatic instruction (see Lüthi 1986: 84).

FORMULA TALES AND CUMULATIVE TALES

Many folk narratives involve the use of verbal formulae. Fairy tales use formulaic opening and closing phrases, such as the familiar 'once upon a time' and 'happily ever after', as well as formulaic rhymes such as 'Fe Fi Fo Fum', and formulaic narrative sequences involving such devices as triadic repetition. In the formula tale, however, the formula, and variations upon it, become the basis of the act of storytelling itself. Typically, the formula tale will establish a simple narrative scenario, and the narrative will develop through the repetition of this formula, sometimes with minor changes or incremental additions. Popular formula tales include 'The Fleeing Pancake' (ATU2025), which is perhaps best known in Britain and North America in a variant that replaces the escaping pancake with a gingerbread man.

A common form of the formula tale is the cumulative tale: a story form in which the central mechanism of the narrative is the accumulation of a list of objects or a sequence of actions. Popular stories of this type include 'The Giant Turnip', 'The House that Jack Built' and 'The Old Woman and Her Pig', the last of which, in the version used by Joseph Jacobs in *English Fairy Tales*, accumulates a dizzying series of eleven events that need to occur before a pig will cross a style and an old woman can get home (Jacobs 1890: 20–23). The 'essential formal quality' of such narratives, Thompson points out, is 'repetition, usually repetition with continuing additions' (Thompson 1977: 234).

Fictions of this sort often have the appearance of being a kind of game, and when told orally, they can operate as a test of the storyteller's memory. They appeal especially to young children, no doubt because of their predictable and repetitive character, and they are, as a result, common fictions in the children's picture book market. In Britain in the 1960s and 1970s the prominent children's book publisher Ladybird included at least eight formula tales in their pioneering series of folk and fairy tales 'Well Loved Tales' (1964–74) adapted by Vera Southgate. More recently a number of children's writers have adopted and adapted the formula tale as a basis for new fictions for children. For example, Julia Donaldson, who has always 'kept an eye out for traditional tales that can be retold', reworked 'an Eastern folk tale about a child who cons a jungle tiger into submission' (McCrum 2004) to create her hugely popular children's picture book *The Gruffalo* (Donaldson 1999, illustrated by Axel Scheffler). *The Gruffalo*, along with its sequel, *The Gruffalo's Child* (2004), is a formula tale as well as a trickster tale that makes a strong appeal to what Elizabeth Wanning Harries has called 'our readerly delight in repetition and in difference' (Harries 2001: 5).

TALES OF FAIRIES AND FAIRY LAND

It is easy to confuse 'fairy tales' with 'tales of fairies and fairy land' because of their shared identification with those supernatural, diminutive creatures so common in British lore. The two genres are different, however. Tales of the fairies invariably and *by definition* include representations of fairy folk, and depict interactions between the 'otherworld' of the fairies and the world inhabited by humans. They often show fairies interfering in human affairs: swapping children with changelings, turning milk sour, leading people astray or confounding lovers; and it is characteristic of the tale of fairies that these confoundings and confusions do not, in the main, end well for the humans involved. Fairy tales, by contrast, do not, despite their name in English-speaking countries, necessarily include fairies, or diminutive beings, of any sort; they do not always deal with an interaction between two realms; and they rarely, if ever, end badly for the people involved. Tales of the fairies also differ from fairy tales in the attitude that the audience of these stories is meant to take to the material: tales of fairies are told as if they might be believed, whereas fairy tales are regarded purely as fiction. For this reason, tales of the fairies must be regarded as closer to legend than they are to fairy tales, which is why neither Briggs nor Aarne and Thompson include them under the category of folk tales.

Tales of the fairies are very prominent in British tradition. Any collection of British folk tales or fairy tales will include several tales of the fairies between its covers. Tales of the fairies have also had a significant impact upon British literature, forming an imaginative substratum for several major works in the canon of English writing, including, most prominently, Edmund Spenser's folklore-inspired allegory *The Faerie Queene* (1590–96), William Shakespeare's *A Midsummer Night's Dream* (c. 1595–96), and John Keats's 'La belle dame sans merci' (1820). Since they are both structurally and historically different from fairy tales, however, the current study does not incorporate an extended discussion of tales of the fairies or fairy land, though readers who wish to know more about fairy lore are recommended to consult *The Fairies in Tradition and Literature* by Katharine Briggs ([1967] Briggs 2002), *Strange and Secret Peoples: Fairies and the Victorian Consciousness* by Carole Silver (1999), *Troublesome Things: A History of Fairies and Fairy Tales* by Diane Purkiss (2000), and, for a focused theoretical study of fairy lore in the Early Modern period, *The Popular Culture of Shakespeare, Spenser, and Jonson* by Mary Ellen Lamb (2006).

JOCULAR TALES

Jocular tales are short anecdotes designed to generate humour. These fictions are usually referred to by folklorists using the German term *schwank* in order to distinguish them from forms of the joke which are not narrative based, such as the pun, and so do not fall under the category of folk narrative. Alongside urban legends and ghost stories, jests or merry tales are the most common form of orally disseminated narrative still current in the developed world today. Fairy tales can sometimes take on the characteristics of a jocular tale. The story of 'The Boy Who Went Forth to Discover Fear' in the Grimms' collection, for instance, includes a 'punch line' that would be equally at home in a joke. The boy in the story, having endured a lengthy and eventful quest to discover how to be afraid, finally achieves his goal on his wedding night when, in an erotically suggestive scene, his new wife pours a bucket of cold water and minnows over him whilst he is sleeping. The fish begin 'flapping all over him', and the boy wakes up crying 'Oh, I've got the creeps! I've got the creeps! Now I know, dear wife, just what the creeps are' (Grimm and Grimm 1992: 20). The joke, in this instance, lies partly in the pun that replaces the shudder of terror with the shudder caused by the physical sensation of cold wriggling fish, and partly in the narrative's rather transparent sexual innuendo.

Whilst fairy tales and jocular stories may coincide, however, there are evident differences between these narrative forms: unlike the fairy tale, the principal objective of the jocular tale is to provoke laughter, and all elements of the narrative are subordinated to this end. Alan Dundes has also argued that certain forms of the joke differ from fairy tales at a fundamental structural level. In the Shaggy Dog story, he argues, the objective of the narrative is to build up the listener's expectations with a long and elaborate narrative and then to disappoint the listener with a deflationary punch line. In the fairy tale, by contrast, 'expectations are almost always fulfilled' (Dundes 2007: 138). This narrative format, Dundes further argues, makes the fairy tale into a narrative form that typically works to reconfirm and validate the end-orientated philosophy of European culture that places high value on deferred gratification. The Shaggy Dog story, by contrast, by using disappointment as its primary mechanism, parodies and undermines the European world-view which holds out expectations of long-term rewards for labours endured. This might be regarded as a characteristic of jokes more generally, since jokes often work through the violation of accepted rules and the parody of agreed cultural standards; fairy tales, when they are not parodies (and therefore jokes of a particular kind), work to confirm accepted rules and to restore cultural standards (Lüthi 1986: 82).

THE NOVELLE

The novelle, sometimes referred to as the novella, is a brief prose narrative, not dissimilar to the fairy tale in form. Unlike the fairy tale, however, the novelle is naturalistic: the events it describes occur in a realistic setting, often at a specified time and place, and the supernatural marvels that occasionally feature in these fictions are, in the otherwise naturalistic settings, treated with incredulity and amazement by their protagonists, rather than with the frank acceptance that is more familiar in fairy tale. Most of the stories written by Giovanni Boccaccio in his fourteenth-century collection of stories *The Decameron* (c. 1350–53) come under the classification of novelle, as do a number of the narratives that were used by Geoffrey Chaucer as a basis for his narrative poems in *The Canterbury Tales* (c. 1380–99). Stith Thompson argues that a large number of the fictions that appear in *The Arabian Nights* should also be identified as novelle rather than fairy tales (Thompson 1977: 8), since unlike the fairy tale familiar in collections from Europe they are given realistic settings (Baghdad or Cairo) and identifiable periods, and since the improbable marvels that are related in the tales will, more often than not, strike the protagonists as occurrences that defy belief. As Thompson suggests, however, the distinction between novelle and fairy tale is not always easy to draw since there is 'much overlapping' between the two categories, and since tales which 'appear in one land with all the characteristics of a novella' may appear in another 'with those of a *Märchen*' (8) (see p. 31 for *märchen* definition). For instance, the English story of 'Cap o' Rushes' is categorised by Briggs as a 'novelle' rather than a fairy tale (Briggs 2002: 88) but narratives which contain very similar elements, such as Charles Perrault's 'Peau d'âne' (Donkey Skin) or 'Cendrillon' (Cinderella), are invariably identified as fairy tales. The differences between these fictions are subtle but, so far as Briggs is concerned, crucial: Perrault's heroines, Donkey Skin and Cinderella, are able to attract the attention of the prince because their appearances are improved by magical means (fairy intervention), but Cap o' Rushes, before going to the 'great dance' presided over by 'her master's son', simply does what any girl might do: she takes off the cloak made of rushes that she uses to conceal her better clothes beneath, and gives herself a wash. Similar as the stories are, the absence of magic in one makes it into a novelle, whilst the presence of magic in the others makes them into fairy tales.

FAIRY TALE

It is this latter feature, above all else, that is often seen to define the fairy tale most exclusively. Folk tales do not necessarily take place in an enchanted environment, nor do incredible events have to occur. In the story of 'Clever Jack' cited above, improbable as Jack's ruses are, nothing of a supernatural character transpires. In fairy tales, by contrast, the magical, in the form of metamorphic transformations, loquacious animals, enchanting spells and improbable feats, is a necessary and ubiquitous precondition. As Stephen Swann Jones observes in his taxonomy of folk narratives, the fairy tale, like other folk narratives, employs 'ordinary protagonists to address issues of everyday life', but the 'essential distinction' that allows us to tell the fairy tale apart from folk narrative is that '[w]hile these other genres of the folktale are reasonably mimetic – that is, they depict life in fairly realistic terms – *fairy tales depict magical or marvellous events or phenomena as a valid part of human experience*' (Jones 2002: 9).

The fairy tale, however, does not practise just any kind of magic. Jones's distinction, here, recalls the discussion of fairy-tale magic in Tzvetan Todorov's classification of the different forms of fantasy writing in his seminal work *Introduction à la littérature fantastique* (1970) [*The Fantastic: A Structural Approach to a Literary Genre*, 1971]. Here, Todorov identifies three basic genres of fantasy writing, distinguished from one another by their approach to the magical: the uncanny, the fantastic and the marvellous (Todorov 1975: 24–57). A piece of fiction is 'uncanny', according to Todorov's reinscription of Freud's term, when the supernatural events that have been described become rationally explicable for the reader, as for instance occurs in the Gothic novels of Anne Radcliffe and Clara Reeves (41). The marvellous arises when the reader decides that no rational explanation is available for the events represented, and 'new laws of nature' must therefore 'be entertained to account for the phenomena', as transpires in the novels of Horace Walpole or Charles Maturin (41–42). Finally, the 'fantastic' occurs when the reader is made to hesitate between a realistic and a supernatural explanation for the events described, a balancing act sustained with mastery by Henry James in *The Turn of the*

Screw (1898). It will often be the case, Todorov observes, that 'the uncanny' and 'the marvellous' involve 'the fantastic' at some point, since these forms of fiction will characteristically suspend the reader in a state of uncertainty for a period of time before resolving their magic one way or another. In the purest form of 'the uncanny', however, the reader will know from the start of the narrative that the events depicted are rationally explicable. Conversely, in the purest form of 'the marvellous' the reader, like the characters, will know from the start of the narrative that events are rationally inexplicable. Fairy tales, in Todorov's schema, fall into this latter category because the reader knows from the outset that normal rules do not apply (54). There is no moment of hesitation for the reader between explanations (is the cat talking or is it an illusion?), and there is no ultimate realisation that apparently supernatural events admit of a rational explanation (I was on drugs when I saw that cat talking). Rather, fairy-tale magic entails an acceptance, from the 'once upon a time' to the 'happily ever after', that magic is normative in fairy land, and that the ordinary rules are suspended. The cat just talks.

The term 'fairy tale' arrived in England as a literal translation of the French *contes des fées*, first used by the French author of fairy tales, Marie-Catherine Le Jumel de Barneville, Comtesse d'Aulnoy, in the title of two volumes published in 1697 and 1698: *Les contes des fées*. A selection of these tales was translated into English under the title *Tales of the Fairies* in 1699, and this was followed by a further volume of *Tales of the Fairies* in 1707 and by *The History of the Tales of the Fairies* in 1716. According to the Oxford English Dictionary, the first recorded use of the specific formulation 'fairy tale' in English was in a casual aside in a letter from Horace Walpole dated 3 May 1749, though there is a better example of its use in that same year in the novel *The Governess* by Sarah Fielding in which a story titled 'The Princess Hebe: A Fairy Tale' is used by a governess to support the education of her young charges. Initially, it seems, the term was applied primarily to the elegant literary tales produced by d'Aulnoy and her circle. In the course of time, however, the phrase has come to be applied to all stories that are comparable, however distantly, to d'Aulnoy's, including those of the Brothers Grimm, which were translated into English by Mrs H. B. Paull in 1868 as *Grimm's Fairy Tales*, and have been referred to as 'fairy tales' ever since in English-speaking countries, even though the German title of this collection, *Kinder- und Hausmärchen*, makes no mention of fairies. Indeed, Edgar Taylor, the first translator of the tales into English, gave them the more accurate title of *German Popular Stories* in 1823.

Some folklorists have lamented the inadequacy of the term 'fairy tale'. As J. R. R. Tolkien has pointed out, it is far too narrow to properly describe the genre it purports to identify, because 'fairy-stories are not in normal English usage stories *about* fairies or elves' (Tolkien 1964: 15). In international folklore scholarship, therefore, the German term *märchen* (pron: mer-<u>k</u>ən) is generally preferred to fairy tale since it is technically more accurate, and since it offers greater opportunity for further dis-criminations. *Märchen* translates literally as 'short tale' or 'short report' and is a diminutive form of the old High German *mär*, meaning 'news' or 'tidings'. The term is frequently used loosely to describe folk and fairy tales of various kinds; but it can also be combined with a series of prefixes to make subtler distinctions between varieties of tale. *Volksmärchen* (literally, people's tales) is used to designate fictions that are relatively close to their traditional roots; *Buchmärchen* (book tales) indicates stories with traditional roots that have been heavily reshaped by known and named authors in the course of their preservation; *Kunstmärchen* (art tales), finally, are fictions in which an author has either (a) used a *märchen* and/or *volksmärchen* as a basis for literary invention but re-written and re-worked it so substantially that it is made into a short story or a novel, (b) invented a narrative that is designed to resemble tradi-tional tales in some respects but that is in fact entirely original, or (c) created an original tale but made substantial use of 'motifs' common in traditional tales.

The term *volksmärchen* usually designates stories collected directly from oral tellers by folklorists and anthropologists; *Buchmärchen* designates those amphibian fictions that inhabit the murky hinterland between tradition and literature, as evidenced in the collections of Giambattista Basile, Charles Perrault and the Brothers Grimm; and *Kunstmärchen* are those tales that are indisputably literary, and carry with them the distinctive style of a named author. The stories of Hans Christian Andersen, Oscar Wilde and George MacDonald generally fall into this latter category, as do the gothic fairy tales of E. T. A. Hoffmann, the philosophical *märchen* of Herman Hesse, and the 'stories about fairy stories' (Carter 1997: 38) written by the twentieth- and twenty-first-century re-writers of fairy tales, Angela Carter (1979), Tanith Lee (1983), A. S. Byatt (1994), Emma Donoghue (1997), Kelly Link (2001, 2005) and Kate Bernheimer (2010).

Useful as these technical terms are for folklorists, however, they have had little impact on general parlance, common usage, as ever, having proved more powerful than logic. 'Fairy tale', for better or for worse, is a term that is widely understood and accepted in English-speaking countries and is, therefore, the term that I have used throughout this book, except where some more subtle discriminations are required. It is perhaps also worth noting that there is a case to be made for the claim that the phrase 'fairy tale' is not as misleading as its critics have suggested. Stephen Swann Jones mounts a satisfying defence of the terminology by arguing that the word 'fairy' is appropriate because it is a metonymic signifier of the magical realm in which fairy tales take place, not a reference to the paranormal entity (Jones 2002: 9). Jones follows Tolkien in this, who, in his essay 'On Fairy Stories' (1947), argues that the word 'fairy' in 'fairy tale' refers not to 'fairies or elves' but to '*Faërie*, the realm or state in which fairies have their being' which may contain 'many things besides elves and fays' (Tolkien 1964: 15). 'The definition of a fairy story', Tolkien adds, does not 'depend on any definition or historical account of elf or fairy, but upon the nature of *Faërie*: the Perilous Realm itself, and the air that blows in that country' (16).

What, then, is the air that blows in that country like? For most readers, the basic plot of the fairy tale will already be familiar. A fairy tale typically deals with the experiences of a youthful protagonist engaged on a journey, or in a series of tasks and trials, that has been necessitated by a change in his or her status: the death of a parent, or the loss of a magical object. This journey or series of tasks takes place in an imaginative environment, peopled by strange beings and wonderful creatures, some of which prove helpful, and some of which become hazardous threats (Buchan 1990: 979). Almost invariably, the progress of the hero is hindered by the actions of a dangerous opponent, such as a witch, an ogre, a wolf, a tyrant king, or a malignant stepmother, but equally invariably (that is to say, almost but not quite) the hero or heroine overcomes his or her opponent, completes the journey or the set of tasks, and, in so doing, secures for himself or herself a more comfortable life, and a more socially eminent position than seemed possible at the start of the story. Not all fairy tales fulfil exactly this pattern, and the phenomenal imaginative richness of this genre is such that even when this pattern is fulfilled, it takes such varied and inventive forms that it is sometimes difficult to map a fairy tale onto this bald schema. Nevertheless, this pattern occurs with remarkable regularity in fairy tale, and almost all the fairy tales which might be considered classics of the genre conform to this model.

It is not the pattern alone that defines the fairy tale, however, for there are a number of narratives that might adopt this plot-pattern without necessarily being fairy tales. Many novels, for instance, including those in Tolkien's own *Lord of the Rings* trilogy (1937–49), conform to the above plot-pattern. It is necessary, therefore, to add that the fairy tale is a short fiction, that it is in prose rather than verse, that it is anonymously authored and collectively owned and that it is, as observed above, a fiction in which magical beings and magical events are normative. The German scholar Max Lüthi in his influential works on fairy tales *Once Upon a Time: On the Nature of Fairy Tales* (trans. 1970) and *The European Folktale: Form and Nature* (trans. 1982) also asserts that the fairy tale is a narrative form in which plot developments, characters, and settings are presented in a formulaic and one-dimensional manner, rather than in a realistic or rounded manner (Lüthi 1976: 47–57; Lüthi 1986: 11). The interior life of a protagonist of fairy tales, Lüthi argues, is rarely described in detail, psychological motivations and emotional responses are explored minimally if at all, landscapes are rarely filled out, and descriptions of only the most basic kinds are used. In sharp distinction to genres such as the novel, therefore, the *märchen*, in Lüthi's formulation, 'siphons off all three-dimensionality from objects and phenomena and shows them to us as flat figures and figured events' (Lüthi 1986: 23):

> In its essence and in every sense, it lacks the dimension of depth. Its characters are figures without substance, without inner life, without an environment; they lack any relation to past and future, to time altogether.
>
> (Lüthi 1986: 11)

In claiming this, he is not arguing that the folk tale is a superficial form, or that it is incapable of being meaningful. On the contrary, Lüthi argues that the 'abstraction' and 'sublimation' that characterises the *märchen* make it into a genre that is capable of addressing fundamental human experiences at a basic and 'universal' level. The generalising style of the *märchen*, as Lüthi expresses it:

> is the prerequisite for the folktale's ability to encompass the world. Only thus is the epic-like short form of the folktale able to become all inclusive. No realistic, individualising portrayal would be able to achieve such universality.
>
> (Lüthi 1986: 79)

Folklorists and scholars who agree with Lüthi's formulation have sought to explain the abstracted style of fairy tales in various ways, depending on their philosophical and theoretical outlook. Lüthi believes that the *märchen* 'realises its own form' in order that it can 'reflect and satisfy certain needs of the human psyche' (Lüthi 1986: 108). Jungian theorists, comparably, argue that folk and fairy tales take the regular and recurrent forms they do because they are embodiments of **archetypes** in the **collective unconscious** that are manifested in all human cultural productions (see Campbell 1993: 17–20). There are also scholars who regard folk and fairy tales as consistently structured because they are encoded representations (or sometimes 'survivals') of rituals used in tribal culture to mark moments of transition in human life. The folklorist Arnold van Gennep described these moments of transition as 'rites of passage', and argued that it is possible to observe the basic structure of the rite of passage, 'separation-transition-incorporation', in cultural practices throughout the world (see van Gennep in Dundes 1999: 99–108). Joseph Campbell, following in the footsteps of both Jung and Gennep, applied this observation to myth and folk tale specifically, arguing that all myths consist of a pattern of 'separation or departure', 'the trials and victories of initiation', and 'return and reintegration with society', because this is the structure of the archetypal 'monomyth' that gives shape the adventures of the human soul (see Campbell 1993: 3–46).

These interpretations, in different ways, emphasise the idea that fairy tales are profound fictions that reflect deep psychological and social experiences. There is another class of interpretation, however, that explains the form of the *märchen* by more mechanical means. Advocates of an exclusively literary invention and dissemination of fairy tales propose that formulaic repetition in fairy tale is the result of literary imitation and mechanical reproduction in print culture (Bottigheimer 2009: 106–7). By contrast, proponents of the view that fairy tales are a tributary of oral tradition, argue that fairy tales have consistent patterns because the conditions of oral transmission have imposed upon them a regularised and formulaic structure (see Olrik in Dundes 1999: 87–97; and Rosenberg 1991: 25–38). According to this view, storytellers, in transmitting narratives, tend to use simple formulae as a basis for their tales, and when stories are remembered and passed on, it tends to be the basic structural formula that is retained, whilst the details of the narrative are freely adapted.

TWO GENRES?

Lüthi's description of the fairy tale as a narrative of 'delightful clarity' which avoids 'unessential details' and seeks instead 'definiteness' and 'firmness' (Lüthi 1976: 50–52), a description which is in turn derived from the Romantic conception of fairy tales as spontaneous and simple eructations of natural wisdom, has proved extremely tenacious. It is a persuasive description if we have in view the pared-down, economic 'folk' style of the Grimm tales, or the gnomic and slim-line fictions shaped by Charles Perrault at the end of the seventeenth century. Those who read widely in the genre of fairy tale, however, will know that there are many fairy tales in the approved canon that do not conform to this description. For example, the fairy tales of Giambattista Basile, which are generally considered to be amongst the first literary fairy tales, are not 'depthless', 'abstract' or 'one-dimensional', but baroque, elaborate, extravagant and sophisticated. Likewise, the stories of Perrault's contemporaries d'Aulnoy, Charlotte Rose de la Force and Marie-Jeanne Lhéritier, in whose company Perrault emerges as the exception rather than the norm, are not restrained and economical, but complex in form, erudite in expression and self-conscious in their treatment of fairy-tale motifs. In the fictions of all these writers, in direct contrast to the Perrault-Grimm proto-type, settings are described in detail, motives are examined and commented upon, and characters are given psychological complexity.

Advocates of the idea that the fairy tale is necessarily a minimalist and rudimentary form would no doubt claim that the stories of Basile, d'Aulnoy and others are not properly speaking fairy tales but *Kunstmärchen* that have become detached from the narratives' oral-folk origins, and therefore no longer express the characteristics of the 'authentic' tradition. There are three diffi-culties with this response, however. The first is that it effectively excludes from the category of 'fairy tales' narratives that most readers would unhesitatingly identify as such and therefore fails to reflect an empirical conception of what this genre is. The second is that it relies upon an unsupportable assumption that a clear distinction can be made between oral and literary traditions. The third problem is that it presents Grimm and Perrault as being the 'authentic' mediators of the fairy-tale tradition, when evidence increasingly shows that Grimm and Perrault did as much to fabricate their model of the fairy tale as any other writer in the genre and therefore have no greater claims to being writers of authentic traditions than other authors of fairy tales. Perrault, as Lewis Seifert (1996) and Harries (2001) have shown, reworked the stories he published in order to make them appear to be the product of simple old peasant women. The Grimms, likewise, remodelled the stories that came into their hands in order that these stories might conform more exactly to the conception of the folk tale celebrated by Romantic writers (see Ellis 1983 and Harries 2001). The tales are thus, in the terminology that Harries borrows from the study of antiques, 'distressed' to look old, in the same way that 'a supposedly antique pine chest' can be 'distressed' to give it the appearance of being much older than it is (Harries 2001: 4).

With such arguments in mind, Harries concludes, it is perhaps better not to think of the fairy-tale tradition as being divided into more 'authentic' fairy tales that are closer to oral tradition and less 'authentic' fairy tales that reflect a sophisticated literary tradition, and to think instead, more simply, of two dominant traditions of fairy-tale writing, existing alongside each other, intertwining and separating at different points of their history: 'one the compact model Perrault and the Grimms favoured; one the longer, more complex, and more self-referential model' that can be seen in the work of Basile, d'Aulnoy, Andersen and Carter (Harries 2001: 16). Tales in the former tradition, Harries writes, have a 'carefully constructed simplicity' that 'works as an implicit guarantee of their traditional and authentic status'; tales in the latter 'work to reveal the stories behind other stories' and so are 'determinedly and openly "intertextual" and "stereophonic"' (17). But '[n]either model of the tale is new'. Both traditions have long genealogies, both engage in a blending of oral and literary influences, and both, therefore, are representative of the diverse genre of the fairy tale.

NOTES

1 See 'Tale Type' in Glossary.
2 See 'Tale Type' in Glossary.

2

THE EMERGENCE OF A LITERARY GENRE

EARLY MODERN ITALY TO THE FRENCH SALON

TOM TIT TOT: THE AUTHORISATION OF TRADITION

As a child, the Victorian poet Anna Walter Thomas (née Fison) lived in Suffolk, the youngest of 20 siblings by two mothers. Her parents disapproved of fairy tales, believing that they would 'excite [their children's] fancy too much'; but the children, being too many for strict regulation, had no difficulty in evading parental strictures on their entertainment (Williams n.d.: 7). They ran wild in the woods, inventing strange fairy rituals; and they fed these rituals with the stories that had been told them by servants. One of these tales was 'Tom Tit Tot' – the story of a sinister imp with a twirling tail, who, like the German character Rumpelstiltskin, gives assistance to a benighted heroine, but then loses the prize he has demanded after the heroine is able to learn his name.

Another was the story of 'Cap o' Rushes', a Suffolk Cinderella who, having failed to express her love for her father in sufficiently ardent terms, is ejected from the family home, and must work in degrading circumstances before she is finally discovered by 'the master's son'. In 1871, Anna Fison married the Reverend Walter Thomas, and moved to Bangor in Wales where, as well as becoming a 'capable coadjutrix' of her hard-working husband (Williams n.d.: 19), she added to her considerable skills as a linguist by mastering Welsh, and composing several prize-winning Welsh-language poems. She maintained her Suffolk connections, however, and when in the late 1870s the folklorist Francis Hindes Groome started making enquiries about Suffolk storytelling for the 'Suffolk Notes and Queries' section of the *Ipswich Journal*, Walter Thomas wrote down dialect versions of 'Tom Tit Tot' and 'Cap o' Rushes', and sent them to him. Groome was delighted with the stories, later observing that they were 'by far the best versions of the old *Folk Lore* hitherto collected in England' (Fison 1899: 5), and published them in the *Ipswich Journal* between 1877 and 1878 where they were read and appreciated by a select circle of the Suffolk literati. The stories then lay forgotten for a time, until, several years later, the noted Victorian folklorist Edward Clodd, whilst 'looking over a bundle of old numbers' of the *Ipswich Journal* (Clodd 1898: 8), came across them, and decided to republish 'Tom Tit Tot' in the eminent organ of the Folk-Lore Society of Great Britain, the *Folk-Lore Journal*, where they appeared in 1889 along with an essay in which Clodd argued that the motif concerning the guessing of a creature's name in tales of the Rumpelstiltskin type is a survival of the primitive belief that knowledge of names gives power. In the *Folk-Lore Journal*, the story was seen by its then editor, the president of the Folk-Lore Society, Joseph Jacobs, who was, by chance, in the process of assembling his own collection of English fairy tales. Recognising, like Groome and Clodd before him, the power and significance of 'Tom Tit Tot', Jacobs seized upon the tale, toned down the dialect, and gave it pride of place as the first story to appear in his collection *English Fairy Tales* (Jacobs 1890). Neither Clodd nor Jacobs were too careful about how they attributed the story, perhaps because they believed it, as a fairy tale, to be a kind of common property. Clodd had noted that the story had been sent to Groome 'by a lady to whom they had been told in her girlhood by an old West Suffolk nurse' (Clodd 1898: 8), and Jacobs had simply observed that the story was '[u]nearthed by Mr. E. Clodd from the "Suffolk Notes and Queries" of the *Ipswich Journal*' (Jacobs 1890: note 1). In Joseph Jacobs's book, however, the story was seen by Walter Thomas, and when, in 1898, Clodd republished an adapted version of his essay on 'Tom Tit Tot' as the book *Tom Tit Tot: An Essay on Savage Philosophy in Folk-Tale*, she seized the opportunity to set the record straight, and did so in the manner customary in the period, through a letter to *The Times*. She wrote:

> Sir, – Though a daily reader of my *Times*, I missed your review of the 18th inst. of Mr Clodd's 'Tom-Tit-Tot' ... Is it too late for me to answer the inquiry there as to the *provenance* of the story? Tom-Tit-Tot was told to me very far back in the fifties by a servant; the dialect was hers, and was then the common speech in West Suffolk. I wrote it down years after, for Archdeacon Groome (or his son), who told me he had sent it and 'Cap O'Rushes', which I also gave him, to the *Ipswich Journal*. Many years after, when I had almost forgotten the circumstance, I found the stories to my astonishment in Mr. Jacobs's book of fairy tales. The dialect was softened; otherwise they were word for word. Mr Jacobs, to whom I wrote, told me that, as they were not copyright, they were his to print; but he was good enough to insert my name on a slip in the book, probably considering ... that the honour of appearing by name in his book was sufficient reward.
>
> (Walter Thomas 1898)

Jacobs subsequently included Walter Thomas's name in the notes of future editions of *English Fairy Tales*; he also makes complimentary remarks about her, under her maiden name 'Miss Fison', in the introductory notes to *More English Fairy Tales* (Jacobs 1894). Even today, however, Anna Walter Thomas is often deprived of due recognition in accounts of the provenance of this story. After Susanna Clarke's superbly inventive reimagining of 'Tom Tit Tot' in her short story 'On Lickerish Hill' (2006), a note appears that reads: 'Among the many sources she drew upon for this story the author would particularly like to acknowledge folklorist Edward

Clodd's wonderful 1898 rendition of *Tom Tit Tot* in Suffolk dialect'
(Clarke 2007: 62). No doubt Anna Walter Thomas is gnashing her
teeth from beyond the grave. Though Walter Thomas's indignation
at having her story seized by the crowd of men that dominated
the Victorian Folk-Lore Society is understandable, however, her
insistence on being known as the named author of this story
should also, as Neil Philip observes, 'warn us not to regard her
text as the simple, faithful transcript it appears' (Philip 1992:
116). Quite the contrary, Walter Thomas's artful shaping of this
story suggests the operations of a sophisticated scribe, and her
proficient imitation of West Suffolk dialect leads us to suspect,
not a disinterested reflection of tradition, but an erudite invention
of it. This view is to some extent confirmed by Walter Thomas's
later career as an accomplished imitator of Welsh dialect poetry,
in which she again becomes, as Catherine Brennan has argued, an
inventor of tradition, taking command and control of the languages
and narratives of the Welsh people in order to assert her 'linguistic
dominance ... as a member of [an English] elite' (Brennan 2003: 193).

This history of 'Tom Tit Tot' tells us a great deal about the
history of fairy tales more generally. Like many fairy tales, this story
has a complex provenance, involving numerous mediators, and
repeated transformations. In the first instance, it is attributed to an
oral source, which encourages us to assume a long, but ultimately
untraceable, root in popular spoken culture. Importantly, however,
it is not the oral source that has survived, but a literary adaptation of
it, which has been subjected to greater or lesser degrees of manipulation. What contemporary readers experience therefore is not the
story in the form it may have taken in oral tradition, but the story as
it has come to exist after a process of literate adaptation and
appropriation.

The provenance of 'Tom Tit Tot' also reveals how profoundly
the transmission of this narrative is determined by issues of power
and access to the resources of culture. The story begins its life in
the possession of a working-class woman, but it is successively
claimed and modified, first by a middle-class woman who gives it
an authorised literary shape, then by middle-class men who
determine that it should enter the fairy-tale canon. In this process, the working-class woman who first narrated this story to the

young Anna comes to play an important symbolic role in the literary fiction: she signifies a romantic idea of the narrative's past and embodies a notion of the story's popularity, but she is no longer the owner of the narrative. She has become part of the idea of the story, and so, in a certain respect, an object within it.

A similar process may be observed in most major European collections of fairy tales, in which it becomes conventional to identify common sources for elaborate literary fictions: Giambattista Basile identifies a panoply of grotesque lower-class female characters as the narrators of the stories in the *Lo cunto*, Perrault attributes his *Contes* to the fancy of his son's nurse, and the Grimms permit sufficient ambiguity in their notes and prefaces to allow the reader to believe that a proportion of their stories issue directly from peasant huts. In each case, the oral sources of the stories are conceded as a literary device in order to promote a certain set of ideas about the fiction: Basile uses his exaggeratedly comical storytellers – women with names such as 'shitty Iacova', 'drooling Antonella' and 'snout-faced Ciulla' (Basile 2007: 42) – to conjure the image of a bawdy street culture that can be used as a weapon against the stuffy aristocratic court; Perrault uses his son's nurse as a mask that allows him to tell the entertaining and artless stories of the peasantry whilst simultaneously maintaining a courtier's aloof poise; and the Grimms use the idea of peasant storytellers to give shape to a politically and socially useful concept of a durable national folk. But in all instances, the oral storyteller in these fictions is not represented for her own sake, but becomes a vehicle for the objectives of the story's literate mediators. Though these stories may have survived for long periods of time in the mouths of poor women, therefore, they are, as we apprehend them now, the products of a middle-class appropriation of this working-class culture, and they are borne out of an attitude to that source culture that seeks to romanticise it, but simultaneously to hold it at arm's length.

THE DEVELOPMENT OF A GENRE: ANTIQUITY TO EARLY MODERN ITALY

In its literary form, the story of 'Tom Tit Tot' is relatively young for a fairy tale: it first enters the literary record in 1871, and becomes part of the agreed canon of English fairy tales in 1890. Even if we regard this story as a regional variant of the international **tale type** ATU500 ('The Name of the Supernatural Helper') we are not able to trace it back very much further into history: the earliest manifestations of the tale type appear in the seventeenth century as the story 'Ricdin-Ricdon' in Madame Lhéritier's collection *Bigarrures ingénieuses* (1696) and as 'Le sette cotennine' ('The Seven Pieces of Bacon Rind') in Giambattista Basile's *Il Pentamerone* (1634). For many other fairy tales, it is possible to demonstrate far greater antiquity. The earliest recorded narratives that resemble the kinds of fiction that might today be identified as fairy tales begin to appear in writing between 1,250 and 2,000 years before the birth of Christ on ancient Egyptian papyri, where it is possible to find distant but nonetheless recognisable variations on stories such as 'The Two Brothers' (ATU303) (see Thompson 1977: 273–76; and Lang 1913: II. 318–20). Thereafter, narratives of fairy tales can be found anticipated in Babylonian and Assyrian writings (see Thompson 1977: 276–78), in the classical literatures of Ancient Greece and Ancient Rome (see Anderson 2000), in the Great Sanskrit texts of ancient India, in Norse sagas and Anglo Saxon epics, and in the chivalric Romances of medieval Europe. To give just three examples: the story of a grateful dead man (ATU505), which appears as Hans Christian Andersen's 'The Travelling Companion' in 1835 and in George Peele's play *The Old Wife's Tale* in 1595, can be traced back at least as far as the apocryphal *Book of Tobit* from the second century BCE (see Gerould 1908); elements of Giambattista Basile's early-seventeenth-century story 'Petrosinella', in which the daughter of an ogre aids a hero in his flight from her father (ATU313), are found in the story of 'Śringabhuja and the Daughter of the Rākshasa' (Book 7, Chapter 39) in the eleventh-century Sanskrit collection the *Kathasaritsagara* (*The Ocean of Story*) written by the Kashmiri court poet Bhatta Somadeva (Somadeva 1968: III, 218–39); and Basile's story of 'Sun, Moon and Talia', which reappears as 'Sleeping Beauty' in Perrault's *Contes* of 1697, may be traced back to two anonymous fourteenth-century prose romances: *Perceforest*, from France, and the Catalan romance *Frayre de Joy et Sor de Plaser*. Fairy tales, on this evidence, have a history that is as broad and as long as human culture itself: they have fed the literary imagination for as long as pen is able to record, and have been disseminated throughout the world along the many and complex lines of human intercultural communication. Even as we observe that fairy tales have profound roots, however, we simultaneously become aware that the presence of these stories in older texts does not necessarily indicate the presence of fairy tale as a recognisable genre. In these older settings, the stories that we now identify as fairy tales appear, not in a form that we would recognise as belonging to fairy tales, but in other generic guises: they appear as animal fables, as episodes in long chivalric romances, as passages in epics, as religious parables, as fragments of myths, as realistic novellae, as poetic sagas, as naturalistic folk stories, as tales within tales embedded in Indian and Middle Eastern narrative cycles – but rarely if ever do these early fictions have the stylistic properties, the formal shape, the recognisable characters, the distinctive languages, associated with the modern European fairy tale as described in the previous chapter. Perhaps equally importantly, none of these fictions are *coded* as narratives belonging to the same type, as they come to be when they are assembled together in later years under the unifying banner of 'fairy tale'. Our understanding of the age of the fairy tale, in this respect, must depend upon what we conceive the fairy tale to be: if fairy tales are defined by their stories, then they are as old as written records can show; but if fairy tales are defined by form, style, and generic coding as well as story, then the fairy tale does not emerge until relatively recently in narrative history.

Precisely when this happens is a problem that is subject to all the frustrating imprecision that usually attends descriptions of cultural shifts that are, by nature, messy, incremental, and diffuse. According to Nancy Canepa (1999: 15–17; Canepa 2007: 12–15) and Jack Zipes (2001: 846–52) the beginnings of the formation of fairy tale *as a genre* may be traced roughly to those Italian *novella* writers from between the later fourteenth century and the later sixteenth century who, innovating upon the model of short-story writing pioneered by Giovanni Boccaccio in *The Decameron* (1349–50), began to produce collections in which naturalistic novella-type stories in the mode of Boccaccio were increasingly accompanied by stories of magical transformation derived from popular culture. Following the publication of Boccaccio's *Decameron* in mid-fourteenth-century Florence, the novella form had flourished in Europe, the first half of the sixteenth century in particular witnessing 'an explosion of the popularity of the genre amid a reading public whose size and avidity for *novità* [novelty] ... were growing' (Canepa 2007: 12). According to Bruno Porcelli, this popularity was in part motivated by the novella's capacity to function as 'the ideal genre for satisfying the Renaissance curiosity towards the human being in his or her multifarious social roles':

> Renaissance individualism, which expresses itself in a predominantly bourgeois social context, finds gratification in the novella collections ... because they feature ... man, good and bad, with his virtues and defects, as the protagonist of history.
>
> (Quoted in Canepa 1999: 54)

As the form's popularity grew, however, novella writers began to adapt the model, augmenting 'the traditional Boccaccian repertoire of *beffe* and amorous intrigue more and more with motifs borrowed from ... chivalric epics and folklore' – especially 'motifs and compositional devices common to the fairy tale' (Canepa 2007: 12 and 14). To begin with, this process was sporadic, producing occasional fairy tales in collections such as *Il Pecorone* by Giovanni Fiorentino (1378 and 1385) and *Novellae, fabulae, comoedia* by Girolamo Morlini (1520) (see Zipes 2001: 507–11 and 336–37). From the mid-sixteenth to the early-seventeenth century, however, fairy tales began to occupy a more significant place in Italian writing. Two major works of Early Modern Italian fiction consolidate this process. The first is the story collection *Le piacevoli notti* (variously translated as *The Pleasant Nights*, *The Delectable Nights*, or *The Facetious Nights*) published in Venice in two volumes in 1550 and 1553 by Giovan Francesco Straparola (c. 1485–1556); the second is Giambattista Basile's masterwork, *Lo cunto de li cunti, overo Lo trattenemiento de 'peccerille* (*The Tale of Tales, or Entertainment for Little Ones*), otherwise known as *Il Pentamerone*, written in Neapolitan dialect in the early years of the seventeenth century and published posthumously between 1634 and 1636. Both these collections follow *The Decameron* in using a framing device. Straparola's *piacevoli notti* begins with a description of a group of aristocrats who, having been banished for political reasons from Milan, establish a court-out-of-court on the island of Murano, and decide to entertain themselves for the duration of the Venice Carnival by gathering together every evening to beguile 'the fleeting hours' with 'pleasant and gentle diversions', one of which is the telling of stories (Straparola 1894: 5–6). Over the 13 nights of carnival, five of the ladies in the company tell a story each, with occasional additions by the gentlemen, until 74 stories of mixed generic character have been told in total. Basile's *Lo cunto*, comparable at least in its use of a frame tale, opens with a narrative in which the princess Zoza, having been deprived of her beloved, Prince Tadeo, by a 'cricket-legged slave girl' (Basile 2007: 39), uses a magic doll to inspire her rival with an unconquerable desire to hear stories. Ten of 'the most expert and quick-tongued' storytellers in the city are assembled to entertain the slave girl (Basile 2007: 41), and each of these female narrators tells one story per day for five days until, by the conclusion of the fifth day, 50 tales have been told (hence *Pentamerone*). Forty-nine of these stories are independent narratives; the fiftieth story, told by Zoza, concludes the frame tale, for in it Zoza uses the opportunity provided by storytelling to reveal the perfidious actions of the slave girl in obtaining the hand of the prince. On hearing this story, Tadeo has his false bride buried alive and marries Zoza instead.

The tradition of *The Decameron* breathes through both these collections in their uses of a **frame story**, in their presentation of storytelling as one of a number of pastimes, and in the device of an ordered sequence of tale-telling on successive days or nights. The character of the stories told by Straparola and Basile, however, also marks a significant departure from Boccaccio's model. In amongst the 74 stories in Straparola's collection, scholars have identified about 15 stories that can be described as literary *märchen*, including early literary variants of 'Puss in Boots' (Night 11, Story 1; 'Constantino Fortunato'), 'Iron Hans' (Night 4, Story 5; 'Guerrino and the Wild Man'), 'The Sorcerer's Apprentice' (Night 8, Story 5; 'Maestro Lattantio and His

Apprentice Dionigi') and 'Beauty and the Beast' (Night 2, Story 1; 'Galeotto' or 'The Pig Prince') (see Bottigheimer 2002). Half a century later, Basile's *Lo cunto* builds upon Straparola's innovation by replacing the naturalistic Boccaccian repertoire entirely with tales of magic and marvels, making Basile, in Canepa's estimation, the creator of the first complete and 'integral collection of authored, literary fairy tales in Western Europe' (Canepa 2007: 1). Crucial to this transition from Boccaccian realism in the fourteenth century to Basile's fabulism at the start of the seventeenth, Canepa argues, is a shift away from the generally confident and optimistic vision that characterises the early Renaissance period towards 'a much more turbulent view of the relationship between man and his surroundings' driven by the Counter-Reformation and by rapidly shifting economic conditions (Canepa 2007: 12). In the course of the sixteenth century, Italy suffered a significant decline in wealth and power as the focus of European trade shifted from the Mediterranean to newly opened transatlantic routes. In Spanish-ruled Naples, moreover, where Basile lived and wrote, this political and economic crisis was intensified by the Spanish monarchy's efforts to exploit their Italian colony 'in a desperate attempt to finance its involvement in the Thirty Years' War' (Canepa 1999: 19). 'These developments,' Canepa writes, 'resulted in increasingly unbearable and unscrupulously managed taxation as well as recurring scarcities of primary foodstuffs, all of which helped to aliment a situation of social unrest and general lawlessness' (Canepa 1999: 19). In this more turbulent social context fairy tale had the advantage over novella on at least two fronts: it offered writers and readers greater opportunity for consoling imaginative flight away from troubling social and economic concerns; but it also offered polemically orientated writers new ways of engaging critically with an unsatisfactory reality. This latter practice is exemplified, for Canepa, in the work of Basile, whose tales are not merely escapist, but use the imaginative invention permitted by fairy tale to both 'parodically disfigure representatives of social and political authority' and to 'figure different paradigms of social interaction where virtuous ingenuity becomes a winning quality' (Canepa 2007: 13). The story of 'Corvetto', for instance, registers Basile's dissatisfaction with corruption in court life by presenting the story of a respectable young man whose 'admirable behaviour' has earned him a place in the heart of the King but 'inspired hate and nausea in all of the King's courtiers' (Basile 2007: 261). These envious courtiers, embittered by Corvetto's good offices, repeatedly try to dispatch him by persuading the weak-minded King to send him on ever-more dangerous missions: first to steal an ogre's enchanted horse, then to steal its tapestries, and finally to steal its palace. On each occasion, the envious courtiers hope that Corvetto will be killed so that they can take his place. Corvetto confounds his persecutors, however, by succeeding in these hair-raising missions, and ultimately by winning the hand of the King's daughter. Thus, the story concludes, 'the rafters of envy were, for Corvetto, the posts that allowed him to launch the boat of his life in the sea of greatness'; his enemies, meanwhile, 'confused and consumed with rage, went off to shit without a candle' (Basile 2007: 266).

On the one hand, this story reflects bitterly on the realities of a court life, experienced directly by Basile as a mid-ranking courtier in Naples. At the same time, however, it strives to correct insufficient reality by allowing Corvetto's goodness to be rewarded. Basile's story, in this respect, exemplifies a characteristic of the literary fairy tale that has proved durable from age to age, and collection to collection: it is a genre that enables writers to hold a mirror up to their society, reflecting the anxieties and preoccupations of the era, but it also furnishes writers with a means of responding to their society indirectly, using the fabulous and otherworldly qualities of the genre as a mask for social satire, and, more affirmatively, as a means of speculating about how things might be different.

Straparola's *Nights* proved a popular success upon its initial publication. The first volume was reprinted after only a year; and the complete edition went into at least 20 reprints in the following half century. Translations followed too, into French and German and, much later, into Danish and English. In French translation, Straparola's *Nights* would go on to inspire the writers of French fairy tales in the late seventeenth century, such as Madame de Murat, who claimed in the 'Avertissement' of her *Histoires sublimes et allégoriques* (1699) that all the fairy-tale writers of her generation were drawing upon Straparola's collection (Bottigheimer 2002: 128), and in German it would be read by the Grimms, whose essay on Straparola recognises his endeavour to create something new, though they complain that, too often, Straparola 'strove to tell his stories according to the prescribed and customary form and did not know how to strike a new chord' (quoted in Zipes 2001: 880). Basile's *Lo cunto* has also had a significant influence upon the work of later fairy-tale writers: the Grimms were introduced to it by Clemens Brentano shortly before they began collecting their German stories and included a long essay about it in the second edition of the *Kinder- und Hausmärchen* (third volume: 1822) in which they recognise that several of the fairy tales in their own collection made their first literary appearance as fictions by Basile (Basile's 'Petrosinella', for instance, is a variant of the Grimms' 'Rapunzel', and 'Nennillo and Nennella' a variant of 'Hansel and Gretel'). More recently, Basile's fictions have also influenced modern counter-cultural fairy tales for adults. Angela Carter's **carnivalesque** comic masterpiece 'Puss in Boots' (1979), for example, owes much to the outrageous Rabelaisian comedy of the *Pentamerone* with its 'bed tricks', its spirited irreverence for authority, and its over-elaborate Baroque metaphors.

Much as Basile's *Lo cunto* has influenced other fairy-tale writers, however, it has not become as culturally familiar as later collections by Perrault and the Grimms. Scholars have suggested several reasons for this: the stories, as Canepa observes, are written in Neapolitan dialect, making them difficult to access; they are also at odds, stylistically, with the pared-down 'folk' style that Perrault and the Grimms were to make a distinguishing feature of the fairy tale in the following centuries. The principal reason that Basile's tales have become relatively unknown in an era when fairy tales have increasingly been associated with children's literature, however, will be obvious to all readers who pick up an unabridged edition of the stories: they are profane, scatological and obscene. In one of Basile's tales, a goose that shits gold attaches itself to the fundament of a prince after he has attempted to use it as an arse wipe (First Entertainment, Fifth Day, 'The Goose'). The prince issues a proclamation that whoever is 'able to remove that pain in his ass would be given half his kingdom, if a man; if a woman, she would be made his wife'. After this pro-clamation 'flocks of people' arrive at the palace to, as Basile notes in a hilarious aside, 'stick their noses into that affair'; but it is not until the owner of the goose, a poor peasant girl named Lolla, comes to attempt the trial that the Prince is released from his torment. 'Hearing the voice of the one who loved it,' Basile writes, 'the goose immediately let go and ran to Lolla's lap, where it cuddled up to her and kissed her, not worrying that it was trading a prince's ass for a peasant's mouth' (Basile 2007: 391). In another story, an ugly and ill-mannered young girl named Grannizia is punished by some fairies she has affronted by having a donkey's testicle stuck to her forehead (Tenth Entertainment, Third Day, 'The Three Fairies'). The description of Grannizia in this story typifies Basile's exorbitant style and carnivalesque outlook. This unfortunate young woman, Basile writes, was:

> the quintessence of all cankers, the prime cut of all sea orcas, and the cream of all cracked barrels. Her head was full of nits, her hair a ratty mess, her temples plucked, her forehead like a hammer, her eyes like a hernia, her nose a knotty bump, her teeth full of tartar, and her mouth like a grouper's; she had the beard of a goat, the throat of a magpie, tits like saddlebags, shoulders like cellar vaults, arms like a reel, hooked legs, and heels like cabbages. In short, she was from head to toe a lovely hag, a fine spot of plague, an unsightly bit of rot, and above all she was a midget, an ugly goose, and a snot nose. But in spite of all this, the little cockroach looked like a beauty to her mother.
>
> (Basile 2007: 281)

It is hard to imagine such fairy tales becoming commonplace in the bourgeois nurseries to which fairy tales were increasingly relegated in the eighteenth and nineteenth centuries. Equally, it is easy to see why the more sentimental and romantic versions of stories such as 'Sleeping Beauty' and 'Puss in Boots' that appear in Perrault's later collection have, over time, become better known than the variants of these fictions that appear in *Lo cunto*. When the prince comes across Sleeping Beauty in Basile's 'Sun,

Moon, and Talia', he cannot restrain himself in the face of her catatonic charms and copulates with her whilst she is still asleep, a detail that Perrault tastefully revises and that Disney showed no appetite to revive. Similarly, after the cat-helper has rendered good assistance to the protagonist Cagliuso, in Basile's boot-less variant of 'Puss in Boots', the prince, ungraciously revealing his peasant stock, orders that her body should be thrown out of a window when he thinks she has died, a reflection, Zipes believes, of the ways in which Basile felt himself to have been used as a middle-man at court, trapped between a venal elite and an ignorant upstart peasantry (see Zipes in Canepa 1997: 176–93). Such unsentimental and sexually direct narrative developments have ensured that, much as *Lo cunto* has had an impact upon later writers of fairy tales, and much as its importance has been recognised by folklorists, Early Modern Italian fairy-tale writing has not supplied an enduring pattern for the fairy tale in Europe. Indeed, as Nancy Canepa observes, *Lo cunto* has remained 'more of a milestone than a literary model' (Canepa 1997: 11). By the time that *Lo cunto* was published, however, the seeds for the next phase of fairy-tale development in Europe were already being planted in the emergent salon culture of seventeenth-century France.

THE SALON FAIRY TALE IN FRANCE

The development of the fairy tale in Enlightenment-era France is generally regarded by scholars as having happened in two distinct stages, or 'vogues' (Seifert 1996: 5). The first vogue extends from 1690 to the death of Louis XIV in 1715, and is characterised by a period of focused experimental engagement with the form of the fairy tale, conducted by a relatively coherent group of socially interlinked aristocratic writers, often working in dialogue with one another through the network of literary 'salons' that flourished in the period. The second vogue occupies the middle part of the eighteenth century (roughly, 1722–78), and is characterised by a shift in the status of fairy tale from experimental genre-in-the-making, to established genre in need of remaking. Thus whilst the first vogue produces a relatively stable model of the fairy tale, the second vogue witnesses a proliferation of the model as a second generation of French fairy-tale writers began to innovate and elaborate upon the generic codes they had inherited.

The first vogue is generally dated from the publication of Marie Catherine d'Aulnoy's 1690 novel *Histoire d'Hypolite, comte de Duglas* which includes the embedded story 'L'Île de la félicité' ('The Island of Happiness'), a subtle philosophical fairy tale that dramatises the conflicting demands of love and duty. It has long been recognised, however, that d'Aulnoy's literary fiction was the culmination of an established aristocratic practice of narrating elaborate courtly tales orally at social gatherings; a pastime which may have begun as early as the 1630s (Zipes 1989: 2), and that was later documented by social commentators such as Madame de Sévigné who, in a letter to her daughter dated 6 August 1677, describes being told by a house guest 'some of the stories that they amuse the ladies with at [the Court of] Versailles' (Lang 1888: xvii). One of these stories concerned 'a Green Island, where a Princess was brought up, as bright as the day' with fairies as 'her companions' and 'the Prince of Pleasure' as 'her lover'. It lasted, Sévigné notes drily, 'a good hour' (Lang 1888: xvii).

Following the publication of d'Aulnoy's 'Island of Happiness', a rash of fairy tales appeared in print between 1691 and 1696, either published singly or embedded, like d'Aulnoy's story, in longer works. In 1691, 1693 and 1694, Charles Perrault issued his fairy tales in verse, 'Grisélidis', 'Les Souhaits Ridicules' ('The Foolish Wishes'), and 'Peau d'âne' ('Donkey Skin'); in 1695 Lhéritier's *Ouvres meslées* was published, incorporating two striking proto-feminist fairy tales, 'Les enchantments de l'éloquence' ('The Enchantments of Eloquence') and 'L'Adroite Princesse' ('The Discreet Princess'), and in 1696 Catherine Bernard's cynical reflection on marriage 'Riquet à la Houppe' was incorporated into her novel *Inès de Cordoue*. From 1696 through to 1701 the first French vogue for fairy-tale writing then exploded into vivid life in a series of groundbreaking collections devoted exclusively to the fairy tale, including Charlotte-Rose de la Force's *Les contes des contes* (1697), Perrault's *Histoires ou contes du temps passé* (1697), d'Aulnoy's *Les Contes des fées* (1697–98) and *Contes nouveaux ou les fées à la mode* (1698), Jean de Mailly's *Les illustres fées, contes galans* (1698), Jean de Préchac's *Contes moins contes que les autres* (1698),

Henriette Julie de Murat's *Contes de fées* (1698), *Les nouveaux contes de fées* (1698) and *Histoires sublimes et allégoriques* (1699), and Louise de Bossigny, Comtesse d'Auneuil's *La Tyrannie des fées détruite* (1701). In this brief window of time, as Lewis Seifert notes, nine *conteurs* (male fairy-tale writers) and seven *conteuses* (female fairy-tale writers) produced over a hundred fairy tales, a prodigious and varied output that served to cement the form as a recognisable genre, and to establish it as a legitimate medium for literary innovation in the eighteenth century (Seifert 1996: 8).

The tales in these collections are courtly and sophisticated; they exhibit the forms of linguistic display and witty eloquence that would have been valued in court circles, and they repeatedly validate courtly manners and courtly models of identity. Princes are polite, intelligent and well-spoken, and have noble passions for hunting. Princesses exhibit gracious naiveté, are good at managing social affairs, and dress in a gallant, but not overly magnificent, fashion; and the fairies, who play such prominent parts in the fortunes of the protagonists, behave like influential patronesses at court who need to be cajoled and flattered if their good offices are to be secured. Though the milieu and the manners are courtly, however, the tales, like the salons from which they issue, also exist at a tangent to court life. They seek to endorse courtly values, but the degree of licence provided by the fairy tale's status as a marvellous form of writing that can be passed off as fundamentally non-serious (for children and for peasants) allows writers of fairy tales to use them as a covert, but also suitably transparent, means of commenting upon, and even in some cases criticising, elements of court culture. D'Aulnoy's 'The Island of Happiness', though it endorses aristocratic social manners, encourages readers to question the emphasis placed on martial valour in courtly models of masculine identity when it depicts the hero relinquishing love in his valorous efforts to pursue evanescent public glory (see Zipes 1989: 6). Likewise, narratives such as Perrault's 'Donkey Skin' and d'Aulnoy's 'Beauty with the Golden Hair' encode warnings to all-powerful monarchs not to indulge their passions at the expense of the state, and not to allow their power to blind them to reason. The poem 'Donkey Skin', for instance, describes the reign of a monarch who is 'the most powerful king in the world' (Zipes 1989: 67). Initially this King has ruled wisely and well: 'Gentle in peace, terrifying in war, he was incomparable in all ways' and '[t]hroughout his realm the fine arts and civility flourished under his protection' (67). After the death of his wife, however, this King conceives a mad passion for his own daughter that leads him into a series of rash deeds, culminating in the sacrifice of a gold-defecating donkey, upon which the wealth and security of his crown depends. The story that follows ultimately describes a process of reconciliation and healing: the daughter flees the court dressed in the donkey's skin, after a period of degradation she meets and marries a handsome prince, and finally she is reconciled with her father 'who had purified the criminal and odious fires that had ignited his spirit in the past' (74). Perrault's message, however, has by this point been deftly conveyed: absolute monarchs should guard against becoming tyrants lest they destroy the peaceful rule they have hitherto enjoyed. In the court of the absolute monarch Louis XIV it would have been unthinkable for a man such as Perrault to give voice to warnings of this nature openly; the fairy tale, however, apparently innocuous, absurd and fantastical, allows Perrault a degree of licence that he would not be allowed in more direct or officially recognised forms of address.

The strain of social and political critique in French salon tales was, as Zipes (1989) and Seifert (1996) have argued, especially pertinent in the closing decades of Louis XIV's rule. From the late 1680s, France had entered a cultural and economic crisis that was threatening to erode the earlier achievements of the Sun King's reign. Costly wars lead to high taxation, crop failure resulted in widespread food scarcity, and Louis, under the influence of his second wife, Madame de Maintenon, became more orthodox in his Catholicism and increasingly hostile towards the *mondain* culture of which Perrault, d'Aulnoy and their contemporaries were a part (Zipes 1989: 5–6; Seifert 1996: 7 and 69–71). This hostility took, as one of its primary focal points, the role played by women in aristocratic culture. In particular, Madame de Maintenon and François Fenelon became vocally critical of the conspicuous role played by aristocratic women in cultural and social spheres, and proposed that women's roles should be restricted to domestic life and orientated towards motherhood (Seifert 1996: 7; see also de

Jean 1991: 141 and 145). A number of the fairy tales published by d'Aulnoy and her contemporaries during this period may be regarded as direct responses to these attacks. In reply to the conservative assertion that women should play domestic rather than public roles, the *conteuses* published fairy tales in which women use social and political authority with tact, moderation and skill, and in which the heroines are complex and wilful agents who endeavour to take some measure of control over their own destiny. Criticism of the restrictive institution of arranged marriage in seventeenth-century France also became prominent in women's fairy tales of the period. Aristocratic women of the era, and indeed men, could expect to be forced into unions with unsuitable partners in order to repair the economic fortunes of their families, or to secure greater social capital, and this pragmatic matrimonial system was a source of considerable misery, especially for the women who were increasingly being expected to fulfil exclusively domestic roles. In the form of the fairy tale, the *conteuses* discovered a mode of writing that could both champion the cause of 'true' elective love and, simultaneously, reveal the damaging effects of enforced unions with unsuitable partners. This theme is especially prominent in the Beauty/Beast stories of d'Aulnoy in which hapless heroines are compelled to marry hideous suitors. In the story of 'The Yellow Dwarf', for example, a mother's promise to give her daughter's hand in marriage to the 'miserable monster' of the title leads ultimately to the death of her daughter and the murder of her true lover. In an inset story in 'The White Cat', similarly, a princess who is forced into an arranged marriage with a monstrous fairy must witness her lover being devoured by a dragon and is herself transformed into a cat. Both stories illustrate the sentiments expressed in the verse moral that concludes another narrative on this theme, 'The Blue Bird': that 'a marriage/ Unblessed by mutual love is wretched slavery':

Better to be a bird of any hue –
A raven, crow, and owl – I do protest,
Than stick for life to a partner like glue
Who scorns you, or whom you detest.
Too many matches of this sort I've seen,

And wish that now there were some king magician
To stop these ill-matched souls at once and lean
On them with force to keep his prohibition.
He must be vigilant and forbid the banns,
Whenever true affection might be slighted.
And Hymen must be prevented from joining hands,
Whenever hearts have not first been united.

(In Zipes 1989: 349)

These arguments derive directly from d'Aulnoy's personal experience. At the age of 15 her mother arranged for her to be married to Francois de la Motte, baron d'Aulnoy, who was then in his late forties and notoriously dissolute. When the marriage inevitably soured, d'Aulnoy became implicated in a plot with her lover, her repentant mother, and her mother's lover to have la Motte accused of high treason and executed. The plot was not successful, however, and la Motte brought counter charges against his accusers as a result of which d'Aulnoy's lover and her mother's lover were found guilty of calumny and executed. D'Aulnoy's mother, meanwhile, fled to England to evade capture, and d'Aulnoy herself was arrested and imprisoned with the third and only surviving daughter from her marriage; an episode that is revisited by d'Aulnoy in the story 'The Good Little Mouse'. D'Aulnoy later escaped and fled to England to join her mother, and after 15 years abroad, possibly working to redeem herself in the eyes of the French government by spying, she was allowed to return to Paris and to establish her salon in the Rue St. Benoit. In the stories and novels that she wrote after her repatriation she returns obsessively to her earlier experiences: heroines are forced into disastrous unions with grotesque partners, lovers are killed and maimed, victims of tyranny suffer extended exile or imprisonment, and, above all, spirited and intelligent women are subjected to the cruel restrictions of patriarchal authority. Sometimes the stories compensate for these calamities by offering a happy ending, but just as often the tyrannical and the monstrous forces of oppression triumph over true love and personal liberty.

The life experiences of d'Aulnoy thus stamp her fairy tales with an attitude that, whilst it couldn't be called feminist in a modern sense, is at least sympathetic to women's concerns. By contrast, Charles

Perrault's slim assemblage of prase tales, which appeared in the same year as d'Aulnoy's first collection, reflects a quite different world view. This collection was published in 1697 under the title *Histoires ou contes du temps passé avec des moralités* (*Stories or Tales of Past Times with Morals*), but the collection also has an evocative frontispiece, depicting an old woman spinning and telling tales to a group of children with a placard on the wall reading *Contes de ma mere l'oye*, from which the stories get their alternative title: *Tales of Mother Goose*. The tales are dedicated to the niece of Louis XIV, Élizabeth Charlotte d'Orléans, and were first published under the name of Perrault's son, Pierre Perrault D'Armancour – possibly because Perrault, like Puss in Boots bringing plump partridges to the King, wanted to give the advantage of the flattering dedication to his son (see also Lang 1888: xxvii–xxxi; Barchilon and Flinders 1981: 84–90; Zipes 1989: 19; and Harries 2001: 29–30). The collection contains a mere eight stories, each with appended verse morals, some of which emerge logically from the tales, some of which are forced or ironic. Four of these stories have come to be numbered amongst the best-known fairy tales in the world: the animal trickster story 'Le Maître Chat ou le Chat botté' ('The Master Cat or Puss in Boots'); the cautionary tale 'Le Petit Chaperon rouge' ('Little Red Riding Hood'), and the classic romantic fairy tales 'La Belle au bois dormant' ('The Sleeping Beauty in the Woods') and 'Cendrillon ou la petite pantouffle de verre' ('Cinderella or The Little Glass Slipper'). Also in the collection is the marital horror story of 'Barbe bleue' ('Bluebeard') which, for obvious reasons, is now less common in collections of fairy tales directed at children; 'La petit poucet' ('Little Thumbling'), which includes gruesome scenes of child murder and cannibalism; the didactic moral fable 'Les fées' ('The Fairies'); and the curious allegorical tale 'Riquet à la houppe' ('Riquet with the Tuft') in which the relative merits of beauty and intelligence in men and women are explored (see Warner 1995: 253–55; and Harries 2001: 35–39).

As a number of commentators have observed, the differences between the style of Perrault's tales and those of the *conteuses* who were his contemporaries are striking. Perrault's stories, unlike those of many of his contemporaries, are short ('Little Red Riding Hood' is a compact two pages); they seek, wherever possible, to exclude needless flights of fantasy and to 'rationalise' incredible

occurrences; and they establish narrative developments in a suc-
cinct and economical manner. This economic style made a direct
appeal to conceptions of the fairy tale that were dominant
between the late-eighteenth and the early-twentieth century,
effectively simulating a model of narration that was increasingly
associated with the folk sources of the tales. Perrault's more
rationalised and morally instrumental fictions also held greater
appeal in Europe in an age in which flights of fantasy could only
be justified if they could also be seen as morally improving,
directed at children, and, paradoxically, as sensible as a literature
of the marvellous could conceivably be. This has effectively ensured
that Perrault's fairy tales have been canonised, whilst the tales of his
female contemporaries, though more in number, have been critically
neglected. In recent years, however, scholars have begun to reassess the canon, and reassess the value of stories produced by
d'Aulnoy and others (see Harries 2001: 19–72). This reassessment
has in part been motivated by a perception of the differences
between the treatment of women in Perrault's tales, and the
treatment of women in tales by the *conteuses*. In Perrault's tales,
the heroines are often passive figures awaiting revival at the hands
of a bold prince (Sleeping Beauty), self-sacrificing models of virtue
and chastity who triumph because of their willingness to conform
to the patriarchal order (Cinderella), or wayward women who
have drifted out of the orbit of patriarchal control and who need
to be chastised for their curiosity or their disobedience (Little Red
Riding Hood, Bluebeard's wife). The heroines of d'Aulnoy, Lhéritier and Bernard, by contrast, remain complex and ambiguous figures: they can be vain, self-interested, and wicked, and they can play
the role of victimised martyrs, monstrous persecutors or models of
goodness, but they can also be intrepid questers, 'smart politicians'
and erudite conversationalists. Most importantly of all, they are
invariably the active subjects in their stories, rather than the docile
objects of male reward, and it is this above all that motivated their
initial neglect as canonical fictions, and their recent recuperation by
feminist scholars.

By the death of Louis XIV in 1715, the *conteurs* and *conteuses* of
the 1690s had either died or, with a few exceptions, ceased literary
activity, and the first vogue was over. By this time, however, an

influential and recognisable model of fairy-tale writing had been established that a new generation of writers had begun to respond to, elaborate, and depart from. Seifert identifies at least seven distinctive forms that the fairy tale took during this second vogue: the oriental, sentimental, philosophical, parodic, satirical, pornographic and didactic (see Zipes 2000: 178). Two of these new strains have had a particularly marked effect upon the development of the fairy tale more broadly. The first is the 'sub-vogue' for narratives that imitate or simulate a certain idea of the 'oriental' tale, initiated by the publication, between 1704 and 1717, of Antoine Galland's enormously popular *Les mille et une nuits*, a translation, and to some extent an adaptation, of the Middle Eastern cycle of stories known as *The Thousand and One Nights* or *Arabian Nights* (see Irwin 1994: 14–18; and Kabbani 2004: 25–26).

A second highly influential development in the fairy-tale writing of eighteenth-century France was the tendency, partly inspired by the tales of Perrault, to instrumentalise fairy tales as didactic fictions that can be used in the moral education and 'socialisation' of children. The most significant figure associated with the latter development was Jeanne-Marie Leprince de Beaumont (1711–80), a teacher and governess who produced a substantial body of instructional literature for the edification of her young charges, including *Le magasin des enfants* (1757; *The Young Misses Magazine*) in which a fictional governess educates a group of young girls by telling them anecdotes, exempla and fairy tales. Included in these fairy tales is the story 'La belle et la bête' ('Beauty and the Beast'), a shortened version of Gabrielle-Suzanne de Villeneuve's novella of the same name from 1740, and the source of most modern versions of this internationally recognised tale. This story, as is well known, concerns a young girl who is sent to a beast after her father has plucked an illicit rose from the beast's garden. At first the girl is terrified by the beast, but over time she comes to see his inner goodness, and finally disenchants him by agreeing to marriage. In de Beaumont's hands, the story becomes a vehicle for illustrating the virtues supposed to be possessed by the gently raised, young bourgeois girl of the eighteenth century: she cares for her father and is prepared to sacrifice her own interests for his; she behaves generously to her sisters even when they are vile to her; she is sufficiently lacking in vanity to value true goodness over good looks; and she triumphs as a result of relentless self-sacrifice and unimpeachable moral probity. In the context in which this narrative appears, the story also becomes of forum for explicating the idea that it is one of the roles of a virtuous woman to humanise and civilise bestial masculinity. Such explicitly ped-agogical approaches to fairy tale, Seifert argues, helped shift emphasis 'away from the genre's aristocratic roots' in the middle part of the eighteenth century, and instead refashioned the genre so that it would increasingly promote the 'complex of bourgeois Christian values that was to be at the core of nineteenth-century children's literature' (Zipes 2000: 181).

3

THE CONSOLIDATION OF
A GENRE

THE BROTHERS GRIMM TO HANS
CHRISTIAN ANDERSEN

GERMAN ROMANTICISM AND THE
BROTHERS GRIMM

The seventeenth- and eighteenth-century French vogue for fairy-tale writing culminated with the publication, between 1785 and 1789, of the 41 volume *Cabinet des fées*, edited by Charles-Joseph de Mayer. This vast anthology of *contes* is both monument to and mausoleum for the French fairy tale: it navigates a hundred-year history of story-writing, extending from early French *conteurs* and *conteuses* such as d'Aulnoy and Perrault, to enlightened philosophical moralists such as Jean Jacques Rousseau and Madame de Beaumont; but it also appeared when that hundred-year history was coming to an end, for shortly after the final volumes of the *Cabinet* were published in 1789 the court culture that had originally nurtured and polished the aristocratic fairy tale of the era was decimated by the onset of the French Revolution. By this time, however, the impetus to collect and rewrite popular traditional tales had shifted to Germany, where an alternative movement was underway, sparked, in part, by an anxiety about the dominance of French fairy-tale models, and motivated by a desire to recover 'authentic' German tales that might reflect an 'authentic' German identity. This movement found its most influential spokesman in the philosopher and poet Johann Gottfried von Herder who, inspired by British publications such as Thomas Percy's *Reliques of Ancient English Poetry* (1765), was arguing that the recovery of an ancient national heritage was a vital prerequisite to the establishment of a coherent idea of the German nation. 'Empire of ten peoples, Germany!' he had entreated the nation in 1777:

> You have no Shakespeare. Have you also no songs of your forebears of which you can boast? ... The voice of your fathers has faded and lies silent in the dust. Nation of heroic customs, of noble virtues and language, you have no impressions of your soul from the past?
>
> Without a doubt they once existed and perchance still do, but they lie under the mire ... Lend a hand then, my brothers, and show our nation what it is and is not.
>
> (Wilson 1973: 828)

This call to spearhead 'a rejuvenating return to origins' (Luke 1982: 20) by collecting the literatures and folk traditions of the German past had a significant impact upon a generation of young Romantic writers in Germany. It motivated Goethe, briefly, to collect folk ballads from Alsace. It also inspired the Romantic authors Clemens Brentano and Achim von Arnim to publish a collection of German *volkslieder* (folk songs) between 1805 and 1808 titled *Des Knaben Wunderhorn: Alte Deutsche Lieder* (*The Boy's Magic Horn: Old German Songs*) (Luke 1982: 20–21). The fullest realisation of Herder's cultural project, however, came with the efforts of the sibling scholars Jacob and Wilhelm Grimm to recover, classify and preserve German traditions in their *Deutsche Sagen* (1816–18; *German Legends*), *Deutsche Mythologie* (1835; *German Mythology*), and, above all in influence and importance, *Kinder- und Hausmärchen* (first edition, 1812–15). In these collections of traditions, as in Jacob Grimm's *German Grammar* (1819–37) and the dictionary of the German language that he began to compile in 1837, the brothers sought to shore up an idea of German nationhood by rooting it in a long past and by giving it a coherent linguistic and cultural identity in the present.

The initial impetus for the Grimms' tale collection came from Brentano and Arnim. Jacob had contributed a handful of songs to the second and third volumes of *Des Knaben Wunderhorn,* and Brentano had asked Jacob and Wilhelm if they would collect some *volksmärchen* for a projected future work concentrating on prose traditions rather than songs. Brentano and Arnim had cast the net wider too, issuing a call for stories in 1805 that resulted in them being sent two narratives, 'Von dem Fischer un syner Fru' ('The Fisherman and his Wife') and 'Von dem Machandelboom' ('The Juniper Tree'), composed in Pomeranian dialect by the artist Philipp Otto Runge. The Grimms embraced the project with their characteristic enthusiasm for scholarly work. From 1806 they began procuring popular traditional tales, primarily from friends and neighbours in Kassel, and by 1808 they were able to send their former lecturer in law, Friedrich Carl von Savigny, and his children, copies of seven stories they had gathered, including a version of 'Rumpelstiltskin' collected from Lisette and Dortchen Wild (the latter, Wilhelm's future wife) and a version of 'Snow White' collected from the 17-year-old Jeannette Hassenpflug. These stories were then incorporated into a manuscript of 56 tales that the brothers sent to Brentano in 1810 as evidence of their progress. Brentano, by this time, had lost interest in the project, and, in a demonstration of his diminishing interest, failed to acknowledge the arrival of the manuscript and later admitted that he had misplaced it; a development that was irritating for the Grimms, but not disastrous, for they had wisely made a copy of the manuscript before sending it. Brentano's carelessness, however, has ultimately been scholarship's gain, for the manuscript he lost in 1810 was recovered in the library of the Abbey of Oelenberg in Alsace in 1920, and has since provided scholars with vital information about the draft stories – a resource that is especially precious because the Grimms destroyed their own manuscript records of the stories they gathered.

In 1809 Arnim had also indicated that he no longer wished to continue with the collection, and handed the stories he had been given by Runge to the Grimms for their own use. The Grimms were thus free to develop the project on their own terms, which, for Jacob, meant endeavouring to maintain a greater fidelity to tradition than had been intended by Brentano and Arnim, who had sought to use folk narratives as a basis for artistic works of their own devising. Despite Arnim's reluctance to remain involved in the project himself, however, he continued to show an interest in the Grimms' work and, during a visit to the Grimms in January 1812, had asked to read the manuscript collection. 'Pacing up and down the room,' Wilhelm later recalled, Arnim 'read sheet after sheet, while a tame canary, keeping its balance with graceful movements of its wings, was perched on his head' (Michaelis-Jena 1970: 50–51). When he had finished reading, he told the brothers that it would be a mistake to delay publication in the interests of 'completeness', since in 'striving for completeness, the job might be given up altogether in the end' (Michaelis-Jena 1970: 50). Taking his advice, the Grimms began to prepare the selection of tales they had gathered for publication, and Arnim, using his connections in Berlin, secured them a publisher.

The first volume of the Grimms' tales, accordingly, was completed in the course of the year, and went to press in December 1812 under the title *Kinder- und Hausmärchen, gesammelt durch die Brüder Grimm (Children's and Household Tales, Collected by the Brothers Grimm)*. The volume comprised 86 numbered tales from various sources, including most prominently: the two stories sent to Arnim by Otto Runge ('The Fisherman and his Wife' and 'The Juniper Tree'); a handful of tales collected from a retired Captain of the Dragoons named Johann Friedrich Krause, who swapped his stories for used clothing; over 20 tales supplied by members of the Wild family who lived near the Grimms in Kassel; over 20 tales from the family Hassenpflug, also in the Grimms' social circle in Kassel; and about 15 narratives from published sources, including 'Rapunzel' from Friedrich Schultz's *Kleine Romane* (1790) and 'The Brave Little Tailor' from Martinus Montanus's *Wegkürtzer* (c. 1557). The first run of these stories was small, only 900 copies, but the reception of the collection was sufficiently positive to persuade the Grimms to proceed with a second volume containing an additional 70 stories, published in time for Christmas 1814 (pre-dated 1815). Two fresh sources of narratives helped shape the distinctive character of the second volume. In 1809, Wilhelm had begun to form a close friendship with the brothers Werner and August von Haxthausen, sons of a wealthy Westphalian landowner. August had supplied a couple of stories for the first volume of tales, but from 1811 onwards Wilhelm enjoyed a series of visits to the family estate at Bökendorf, which led to the collection of a large quantity of fictions from the Haxthausen family and their circle of friends and acquaintances, including, for the 1815 volume, 'The Gnome' (in Paderborn dialect) from Werner's sister, Ludowine, and 'The Worn-out Dancing Shoes' from a relation of the Haxthausen's Jenny von Droste-Hülshoff (Michaelis-Jena 1970: 56–59). All told, this connection led to the acquisition of 66 tales for the Grimm collection (Zipes 1992: 728).

The second new source for the 1815 volume was Frau Katharina Dorothea Viehmann, the widow of a tailor living in the village of Zwehrn near to Kassel whom the brothers had met through their acquaintance Charles François Ramus, a pastor to the French community with which Viehmann was associated. Viehmann, as the Grimms record in the preface to the second edition of the tales, retained a host of 'old tales firmly in her memory' and was able to reproduce them word-for-word 'carefully, confidently, and with great vividness' (Luke 1982: 27). From her they collected 35 tales, including 'The Goose Girl', 'The Clever Farmer's Daughter' and 'Hans my Hedgehog'; narratives that appear more directly concerned with peasant lives than the tales of the first collection collected from young bourgeois women. The Grimms clearly saw Viehmann as a model of the kind of storyteller they wanted their collection to be associated with. A large engraved portrait of her by Ludwig Grimm (another brother) appeared as the frontispiece of the second edition of the tales in 1819, and Viehmann is mentioned by name in the preface to the 1815 edition, one of the few contributors to be credited directly by the Grimms in their published tales. Of course, the reason the Grimms saw Viehmann as being more representative of what they wanted their collection to be than other storytellers was that she was a better embodiment of the idea of the German *volk* than the young middle-class ladies who formed the bulk of their informants. She was in her later years (about 57 when the brothers met her), of relatively low class origins, and her name was suggestive of solid German stock. The Grimms accordingly dubbed her *Die Märchensfrau*, and made her the iconic storyteller of the *Kinder- und Hausmärchen*.

Together the two volumes that comprised the first edition of the Grimm collection contained 156 tales. Over successive editions further tales would be added to this initial store; but already the best-known stories in the Grimm canon were in place, including 'Rapunzel', 'Hansel and Gretel', 'Aschenputtel', 'Little Red Cap', 'The Juniper Tree', 'Snow White' and 'Rumpelstiltskin'. What is perhaps surprising for the modern reader is that this collection of remarkable and highly distinctive narratives did not meet with unmixed approval upon its first publication. Brentano complained that the stories were dull and under-worked, still advancing the claims of his own 'improved' models, whilst Arnim worried that the presentation was too scholarly to appeal to children (Luke 1982: 29; Kamenetsky 1992: 193–94). Parents and educators, meanwhile, expressed concern that the collection peddled dangerous superstitions and was too frightening for children (Luke 1982: 30–31; Tatar 2003: 15–18). Alongside critical responses, however, there was growing evidence that the collection was being read enthusiastically by adults and children alike. Sales at least were sufficient to persuade the publisher Reimer to issue a second edition in 1819. This edition incorporates revised versions of the two previously published volumes, and adds several new fictions to the Grimm repertoire, including 'Faithful Johannes' from Viehmann (who had died in 1815), 'Clever Else' from Dortchen Wild, and 'The Two Brothers' from the von Haxthausen family.

The most interesting characteristic of the second edition, however, is not the new tales it adds but the existing tales it leaves out. As a concession to the concerns voiced by readers about the level of violence in the tales, the Grimms removed some of the more grisly entries, including a particularly brutal cumulative narrative called 'How Some Children Played at Slaughtering' in which the accidental butchery of one brother by another leads to the extermination of an entire family (Tatar 2003: 247). The Grimms also made some of the stories less confrontational for children by transforming the wicked mothers of stories such as 'Hansel and Gretel' and 'Snow White' into wicked stepmothers (Luke 1982: 31; Tatar 2003: 36–37). Also omitted in the second edition of the Grimms' tales are those fictions from the first edition that obviously derive from non-German sources. 'Puss in Boots' and 'Bluebeard', both deriving from Perrault, have been omitted, as has 'Okerlo' which was too close to d'Aulnoy's 'L'oranger et l'abeille', and 'The Hand With the Knife' which was taken directly from a Scottish source. Tales that were related to foreign sources but that had been given a distinctive German twist, however, such as 'Little Red Cap', were allowed to remain.

Five further editions of the *Kinder- und Hausmärchen* followed in the Grimms' lifetime: in 1837, 1840, 1843, 1850 and 1857, and Wilhelm was working on an eighth edition when he died in 1859. The 1857 edition, known as the *Grosse Ausgabe*, or 'Large Edition', contains a total of 210 stories, ten of them religious tales for children, and it is this version of the tales that forms the basis of most modern editions and translations. From 1825 the Grimms also produced a shorter edition (the *Kleine Ausgabe*) of 50 of the most popular stories, illustrated by Ludwig, which went to ten editions in their lifetime, and became standard fare in the nineteenth-century nursery, in which context they functioned to reinforce conventional ideas about family, about German cultural identity and about society.

Comparisons of each of the editions of *Kinder- und Hausmärchen*, and of the published editions with the 1810 manuscript discovered at Oelenberg, show that the brothers, particularly Wilhelm who had effective control of the tales from 1819 onwards, continued to rework the stories throughout their lives, adapting them to make them more aesthetically even, more consistently Germanic, more conventional in their morality, and clearer in character motivations (Luke 1982: 29–30; Zipes 2007: 74–78). The story of 'Hansel and Gretel', for instance, is subjected to serial adaptations, spanning from 1810 to 1857, before it settles into the text we recognise today. These adaptations include, in the 1812 edition, the addition of the character names 'Hansel' and 'Gretel' (in manuscript they are only 'little brother' and 'little sister'), the addition of direct speech, the importation of Christian elements (the children appeal to God twice), the elaboration of the wickedness of the witch, and the diminishment of the father's complicity in the abandonment of the children (Zipes 1997: 42–43 and 46–49). In the 1819 text the 'mother' is then transformed into a wicked 'stepmother'; and in the 1843 text there is a considerable expansion of description and detail throughout (Zipes 1997: 43–44 and 49–50). By the 1857 edition, as Zipes points out, the story is nearly twice the length of the manuscript version (Zipes 1997: 44). Early analysts of manuscripts and editions of the *Kinder- und Hausmärchen* did not regard these transformations as problematic so far as the integrity of the Grimms' claim to be collecting authentic examples of German tradition was concerned (see Ellis 1983: 41–43). In the mid-1970s, however, the German scholar Heinz Rölleke formulated the provocative and discipline-changing argument that the alterations made by the Grimms to the narratives they had collected had materially transformed the aesthetic character of the stories and, in many instances, changed their meaning. In the story of 'Hansel and Gretel', for instance, the exculpation of the father from blame in the abandonment of the children, coupled with the transfer of the blame from a mother to a stepmother, fundamentally alters the source tale, transforming it from a bleak narrative about the threat posed to the child by parents, into a 'domesticated' narrative that preserves sentimental nineteenth-century ideals about the nurturing birth-mother and the just patriarchal authority of the father (Zipes 1997: 50–51).

Rölleke's groundbreaking research into the tales in the mid-1970s also revealed that certain established ideas concerning the Grimms' informants were incorrect. In the 1890s, Wilhelm Grimm's son Herman, on the basis of marginal notations in the Grimms' own copy of the tales, had attributed many of the most important stories in the collection, including 'Little Red Cap' and 'The Robber Bridegroom', to 'Old Marie', 'the housekeeper in the Wild family's pharmacy' and 'an unspoiled, entirely Hessian nursemaid' (Rölleke 1988: 105). Rölleke's investigations, however, demonstrated that the 'Marie' referred to by the Grimms could not have been 'Old Marie' (the dates and forms of attribution are wrong), but must have been the 'young – and by the way very pretty ... Marie

Hassenpflug' born in 1788 into a highly privileged upper-middle-class Huguenot family named Droume, and educated to the highest standards of the day (Rölleke 1988: 106). Far from being an authentic German nursemaid, in other words, this Marie, like the majority of the Grimms' informants, belonged to the same class that the Brothers belonged to. Rölleke also contested the description of Frau Viehmann offered by the Grimms in their 1815 preface as 'a peasant woman from the village of Zwehrn' who communicated 'genuinely Hessian tales'. As the daughter of an innkeeper and widow of a tailor, he observed, she could not be considered a member of the rural peasantry, but in fact belonged to a relatively educated, certainly literate, artisan class. She was also descended from Huguenot immigrants and spoke French as well as German, facts that may explain the 'influence of French fairy-tale collections' on her repertoire (Rölleke 1988: 103–4). In light of such evidence, Rölleke proposed a comprehensive reassessment of 'the field of direct contributors to the Grimm collection'. Contrary to the prevailing view that the Grimms had collected their stories from old German peasant women, the majority of the stories were told by 'very young ladies (between fifteen and twenty years old)' who had 'an excellent command of French' or were 'from families that come from France (the Wild family was from Switzerland)' (Rölleke 1988: 106). Those narratives that did not come from these middle-class contributors, moreover, such as the stories of Frau Viehmann, could hardly be considered to be authentic oral Hessian traditions, as initially claimed by the Grimms, since they were collected from a woman able to speak and read French, and likely to have been strongly influenced by literary traditions from France (Rölleke 1988: 104).

When this research was first disseminated in the 1970s and 1980s it triggered a widespread reassessment, in scholarly circles, of the myth that the Grimms had collected their fairy tales directly from the peasantry, and had left their stories more or less undefiled by touches of artistry. The most sensational expression of this reassessment was John M. Ellis's critical exposé of 1983, *One Fairy Story Too Many*, which advanced the provocative contention that the Grimms had been intentionally fraudulent in their misrepresentation of their collecting practices and in their elision of the extent to which the narratives in the *Kinder- und Hausmärchen* had been rewritten. Observing that the brothers had appeared to intentionally mask the true identity of their middle-class, literate informants by only giving vague indication of the provenance of the stories, Ellis made the explosive claim that the Grimms had perpetrated a hoax upon their public, comparable to the hoax mounted half a century previously by James Macpherson, who, in the 1760s, had assembled the epic poem *Fingal* from disparate sources and falsely attributed it to the ancient Gaelic poet Ossian (Ellis 1983: 96–98). At least Macpherson 'worked hard to collect much genuine material', Ellis asserts:

> [T]he Grimms never bothered to collect material of real quality, lied to their public about its nature and their sources, destroyed their basic material, and again lied about the extent of their own role in creating the text which they published, that role being rather more active than Macpherson's had been. Yet Macpherson generally counts as the faker and forger, not the Grimms.
>
> (Ellis 1983: 98)

In formulating these arguments Ellis exposes a raw nerve of folk-narrative studies: scholars and collectors of folklore in the nineteenth century, in the interests of creating coherent national myths, engaged in a large-scale invention of tradition, homogenising highly disparate narrative materials, and attributing spurious national authenticity to traditions that were, in fact, of complex inter-cultural provenance. In describing the Grimms as literary charlatans who had set out intentionally to deceive the public, however, Ellis overstates the case. Certainly, the Grimms adapted and added to their materials, concealed the extent to which this was done, romanticised their tale-tellers, and promoted an ideal of authenticity that could not be sustained, but they did not invent materials that could not be found in popular tradition, and they did not fabricate any documents. Scholarship today has, therefore, discovered a more subtle explanation. It is now widely agreed that the Grimms substantially reworked their material to suit their own cultural outlook and their own aesthetic standards, and that the stories may, therefore, be read as an expression of the world-view of the Grimms and their social circle. At the same time, however, it is also recognised that the brothers mediated, with a degree of fidelity that was uncommon in the period, traditions that were widespread in popular culture, and that genuine folk tales therefore remain the *sine qua non* of their collection. As Rölleke argues in his riposte to Ellis:

> [F]rom the fact that the Grimms' 'immediate sources' were without exception well-placed members of the middle class or the aristocracy, one should in no way conclude that the stories were transmitted only in these circles and have nothing to say about the common folk, whether in their context or in the manner of their transmission. In all demonstrable cases, when they did not get them from books, the eloquent narrators whose tales the Grimms adapted drew their inspiration from the oral tradition of the simplest people: domestic servants, peasants, herders, and carters. And that is also probably the level of society in which these stories were taken up and passed on. It is only that, in view of our new knowledge about the creation of the Grimms' collection, the manifold filtering to which these tales were subjected must be considered and taken into account.
>
> (Rölleke 1988: 107)

HANS CHRISTIAN ANDERSEN AND THE NINETEENTH-CENTURY *KUNSTMÄRCHEN*

The success of the *Kinder- und Hausmärchen* helped institutionalise a genre that, until the early nineteenth century, had flourished primarily on the margins of literature. By reshaping the narratives until they became more consistently expressive of a bourgeois world-view, the Grimms paved the way for fairy tales to enter into the middle-class nursery as officially sanctioned texts, and by linking fairy tales conceptually to the preservation and perpetuation of cultural identity, they made it not only permissible but desirable for the educated elite – the scholars, historians and social theorists – to begin to show an interest in a form of expression that had hitherto been regarded as beneath the attention of serious men. The result was a growing cultural, creative and intellectual interest in the fairy tale that reshaped attitudes to the genre in the nineteenth century, and that has ensured that it has remained a dynamic element of European literature up to the present day.

As might be expected, the artistic and intellectual responses to the Grimm collection in the nineteenth century were wide-ranging and diverse; but two broad directions in the treatment of the genre may be discerned. On the one hand, inspired by the Grimms' endeavour to draw together an archive of national tradition, scholars across Europe, both amateur and professional, began to make equivalent collections designed to represent, and if necessary to fabricate, the traditional heritage of their own nations, regions and ethnicities. By the end of the nineteenth century, the result of this fruitful process of collection is plain to see in a prodigious and growing corpus of 'national' or 'regional' folklore anthologies which includes Thomas Crofton Croker's *Fairy Legends and Traditions of the South of Ireland* (1825–27), Elias Lönnrot's epic assemblage of Finnish songs, the *Kalevala* (1835–49), Jorgen Moe and Peter Asbjornsen's *Norske Folkeeventyr* (*Norwegian Folktales*, 1841–44), Vuk Stefanović Karadžić's *Srpske Narodne Pripovijetke i Zagonetke* (*Serbian Folktales and Riddles*, 1854), and Aleksander Afanás'ev's *Rússkie naródnye skázki* (*Russian Folktales*, 1855–64). The principal objective of these collections is to preserve, as much as possible, the narrative traditions of a defined set of people at a time when those traditions were felt to be fast disappearing under the pressure of urbanisation and industrialisation.

Simultaneously, however, nineteenth-century novelists, poets, playwrights and storywriters were also engaged in a process of using the tales newly popularised by the Grimms as a basis for the creation of new fictions and new works of art. Fairy tales, for this group of writers, were not, as they were for the folklorists, portals into the past; neither were they a means of reconstructing the world-view of an ancient folk who had polished their stories into anonymity; they were a means of conveying the unique artistic vision of the author, and of expressing complex spiritual, philosophical and moral ideas. This artistic tradition is exemplified by the *märchen* of E. T. A. Hoffmann (see Hoffmann 1992), John Ruskin's *The King of the Golden River* (1851), William Makepeace Thackeray's *The Rose and the Ring* (1855), the stories inset in George MacDonald's 1864 novel *Adela Cathcart* (see MacDonald 1999), Lewis Carroll's *Alice's Adventures in Wonderland* (1865) and *Through the Looking-Glass and What Alice Found There* (1872) and Andrew Lang's *The Gold of Fairnilee* (1888). Preeminent in this tradition, however, is the Danish novelist, playwright, poet and story writer, Hans Christian Andersen, who, in a series of stories published between 1835 and 1872, seized the model of fairy-tale writing that had been established by the Grimms, and reinvented the genre for mid- to late-nineteenth-century audiences.

Andersen was born in the city of Odense on the Danish island of Fyn on 2 April 1805, the son of a shoemaker and a near-illiterate mother. His life story is the prototypical tale of a disadvantaged boy who makes good. At 14, poor and with limited prospects outside of factory work, he travelled to Copenhagen with a handful of savings intent on making his name in the theatre. By the end of his life, as Edmund Gosse records, he had become 'one of the most famous men at that time alive in Europe' (Wullschlager 2001: 5). In letters and autobiographies, Andersen frequently compares his remarkable rags to riches trajectory to that of a protagonist from fairy tale. Like Aladdin, whose story Andersen identified with closely, he began life on the lowest rung of the social ladder and, through a potent mixture of luck, the support of powerful patrons, skill and determination, he ended up associating with those on the highest rung. 'Twenty five years ago,' he wrote to his friend and mentor Edvard Collin in 1844, 'I arrived with my small parcel in Copenhagen, a poor stranger of a boy, and today I have drunk my chocolate with the Queen, sitting opposite her and the King at the table' (Wullschlager 2001: 1). Little wonder that he titled his third autobiography *Mit Livs Eventyr* (*The Fairy Tale of My Life*; 1855). If Andersen's life story is a fairy tale, however, it is a fairy tale with the psychological and social complexity of one of his own self-reflexive narratives, for his transition between worlds, as his biographers have shown, came at considerable personal cost, and even after he had successfully translated himself into the upper echelons of society he retained, throughout his life, the feeling of being an outsider (see Zipes 1983; Prince 1998; and Wullschlager 2001). These feelings of marginalisation emerge in various ways in Andersen's stories. The sentimental narrative, 'The Little Match Girl' (1848), in which an impoverished child match seller gradually succumbs to hunger and cold, expresses solidarity with the oppressed and operates as a form of protest against the conditions of the nineteenth-century poor that is reminiscent of the work of Charles Dickens. In a slightly different generic vein, the story of 'The Emperor's New Clothes' (1837), which Andersen adapted from a medieval Spanish story of Arabic origin, becomes a vehicle for satirising the jaded and corrupted perceptions of a venal elite. Andersen's adaptation of this story typifies his practice. In the original narrative, which appears in Infante don Juan Manuel's collection *Libro de los ejemplos del conde Lucanor y de Patronio* (1335; *Book of the Examples of Count Lucanor and of Patronio*), the fraudulent weavers announce that any man who is unable to see a Moorish king's new clothes is not the truly begotten son of his father (Andersen 2004: 427n). Andersen removes this indelicate plot mechanism, and replaces it with the more socially acceptable notion that the clothes would be invisible to 'any person who was unfit for his position or inexcusably stupid' (Andersen 2004: 91). Anderson also added the detail of the child who is able to pierce the self-deceptions of the adult world, and see things as they are, thus emphasising one of the most recurrent themes in his work: that it is the children, the innocent, the neglected and the unusual who are best able to perceive the truth of the world, not the conventional figures of social authority and establishment wisdom.

Andersen's first fairy tales were published in 1835 in two slim volumes titled *Eventyr, fortalte for børn* (*Tales, Told for Children*). The first of these volumes, issued in the May of that year, contained four stories, three of which – 'The Tinderbox', 'Little Claus and Big Claus' and 'The Princess on the Pea' – were artistic versions of the traditional folk tales he had heard in his childhood in the spinning room of an asylum in Odense where his grandmother worked (Wullschlager 2001: 10 and 144). The fourth, 'Little Ida's Flowers', was an original invention of Andersen's, modelled upon a fanciful exchange between himself and Ida Thiele, daughter of the folklorist Just Matthias Thiele. This story begins with a conversation between a young student who makes paper cut-outs for children, as Andersen himself did, and 'little Ida', who is wondering why her flowers are withered and faded (Andersen 2002: 22). The student tells her that the flowers have been at a ball all night, which is why they are tired, and improvises an elaborate tale in which various kinds of flowers with human characteristics visit a king's castle for a ball. A 'tiresome privy councillor' who is also visiting little Ida, and who does not like the student, is scornful of the story, and wonders 'How can any one put such notions into a child's head? Those are stupid fancies' (Andersen 2002: 25). But Ida's imagination is galvanized by the story, and that night she sees a dream vision of a flower ball in which a yellow lily plays a piano, a birchwood rod dances a mazurka, the forbidding councillor is transformed into a 'little wax doll', and roses become kings and queens (Andersen 2002: 27). The following morning, having allowed the flowers to live in her imagination, she is able to bury them in a stately ceremony, and to look forward to their reappearance the following summer.

This story, as Andersen's first entirely original tale, may be seen as a kind of manifesto for his storytelling: it celebrates the imaginative poet-intellectual who is able to improvise a fantasy that will kindle the imagination of the child; it condemns the arid rationalist who is unable to comprehend the value of fairy tales and who is affronted by the story's refusal to confront reality; and it shows how a child, suitably inspired by a storyteller, is capable of taking pleasure in, and consolation from, enchanting fantasy visions. The story also reveals Andersen's willingness to stoop to the level of the child, in order to see the world from her point of view; a world in which flowers might talk, in which common nursery objects have an animate life, and in which explanations for phenomena such as drooping flowers need not resort to crude science, but may remain poetic and fantastical. Here quite explicitly Andersen rejects the pedagogic rationale for children's fiction; and advances his post-Romantic thesis: that the value of children's fiction resides not in instruction or in facts, but in inspiration and wild fancy.

The second volume of Andersen's stories to be published in 1835 (December) comprised three further narratives: 'Thumbelina' (1835), an original tale that draws together elements from the folk tale 'Tom Thumb' and the E. T. A. Hoffmann story *Meister Floh* (1822; *Master Flea*); 'The Travelling Companion', Andersen's revised version of a traditional Fyn ghost story he had first experimented with in 1830 under the title 'Dødningen' (The Ghost); and a story called 'The Naughty Boy' which reworks a poem about Cupid by Anacreon that had been popularised by Byron in an English translation of 1807 (Robb 2004: 222). 'Almost two centuries on,' Wullschlager notes, 'it is hard to imagine the impact on a child in the 1830s who opened an obscure little volume' and read the innovative, expressive and highly colloquial first lines of 'The Tinderbox':

> A soldier was marching along the high road: Left, right! Left, right! He had his knapsack on his back and a sword at his side, for he had been to the wars and was going home. And on the way he met an old witch. Oh, she was horrid: her bottom lip came right down to her chest.
>
> (Wullschlager 2001: 144–45)

Today, Wullschlager argues:

> [W]e accept imaginative, anarchic stories as the basis of all good children's books, from *Alice's Adventures in Wonderland* and *The Tale of Peter Rabbit* to *Charlie and the Chocolate Factory* and the *Harry Potter* stories. But when Andersen wrote his first fairy tales, children's books were not expected to be about enjoyment: they were usually formal, improving texts which highlighted a moral and were meant to educate, not amuse, young readers.
>
> (Wullschlager 2001: 145)

It was in large part because of the originality of vision in these stories, and their striking colloquial style, that early reviewers were, in the main, hostile in their responses. As Andersen anticipates in the figure of the tiresome privy councillor from 'Little Ida's Flowers', the stories were accused of impeding children's education by filling their minds with fantasy, and were even judged immoral by some. A reviewer in the Danish literary magazine *Dannora* was shocked by Big Claus's casual murder of his grandmother, and by the 'not only indelicate but quite unpardonable' image of a lady being sensitive to a pea that had been placed under her bed. (The literal rendering of the Danish title of the story, 'The Princess On the Pea', according to Alison Prince, is more suggestive than the common English translation 'The Princess and the Pea'; Prince 1998: 163–64.) The response of early reviewers also reveals the originality of Andersen's informal style: 'It is not meaningless convention,' complained *The Danish Literary Times* of Andersen's collection, 'that one does not put words together in print in the same disordered manner as one may do quite acceptably in oral speech' (quoted in Wullschlager 2001: 160). That we would today regard the simulation of oral performance in fiction for children as unexceptionable is in large part due to the revolution in style initiated by Andersen in the 1830s and 1840s.

Despite the critical reception of his early fairy tales, the books were popular with readers and sold well, first in Denmark, then, after their translation into German in 1839 and English in 1846, throughout Europe. Strong sales persuaded Andersen to continue writing fairy tales, so new collections appeared in 1837 (with 'The Little Mermaid' and 'The Emperor's New Clothes'), 1838 (with 'The Wild Swans' and 'The Steadfast Tin Soldier'), 1839 (with 'The Flying Trunk') and, after a one-year hiatus caused by Andersen's trip through Europe, 1841. The tales of 1835–41 effectively comprise Andersen's first period of fairy-tale composition; a period during which he was writing directly to an audience of children and making substantial use of existing folk traditions or existing literary fantasies. From his 1843 collection of tales onwards, however, Andersen began to write more explicitly for a double audience of adults and children, and ceased to rely so consistently upon motifs and plot lines drawn from existing fictions. He marked this transition by naming the collection published 1843 (dated 1844) *Nye Eventyr* (*New Fairy Tales*), and by dropping the subtitle *fortalte for børn*. 'I have now discovered how to write fairy tales,' he wrote to his friend Bernhard Ingemann after completing it:

> The first ones I wrote were, as you know, mostly old ones I had listened to as a child, and which I then usually retold and re-created in my own manner ... Now I tell stories out of my own breast, I seize an idea for the grown-ups – and then tell the story to the little ones while always remembering the Father and Mother often listen, and you must also give them something for their own minds.
>
> (Wullschlager 2001: 228)

In the nineteenth century, a similar model of storytelling was used by Lewis Carroll in the Alice books, by George MacDonald in his fairy tales, and by Oscar Wilde in his story collections *The Happy Prince and Other Tales* (1888) and *A House of Pomegranates* (1891). In some instances, the debt to Andersen is explicit: Wilde revisits Andersen's 'The Little Mermaid' in 'The Fisherman and his Soul' (1891), telling the story of a fisherman who severs his soul from his body in order to enter the sea and live with an enchanting mermaid (see Wilde 1994: 115–48). Before it is detached, the fisherman's soul begs to be able to keep the fisherman's heart, but the fisherman refuses, and so the soul goes into the world heartless, and returns periodically to tempt the fisherman into evil deeds. This story, in some respects, stages a rejection of the central assumptions made in Andersen's narrative. In 'The Little Mermaid', as elsewhere, Andersen advocates, as an ideal, physical self-denial and transcendence of the flesh; the Little Mermaid is made to suffer because of her desire for the Prince, and at the conclusion of the tale, the bodily part of herself must die before she can seek redemption. Wilde, by way of reply, argues that the separation of the soul from the body, and the corresponding segregation of the sensual and spiritual self, will result in the corruption of the soul (see Small 1994: xx–xxi). Despite the philosophical differences apparent between the stories, however, Wilde's willingness to engage in a dialogue with Andersen's fictions is also an indication of a fundamental sympathy in their approach to fairy tales. Both writers rejected the common nineteenth-century model of the moral tale for children that was designed to bully or cajole children into conforming with 'the norms and values of *adult* culture', and sought instead to write from a position of sympathy with the child (Small 1994: xiii); both, moreover, posed a challenge to the conventional notion that it is the role of the adult to civilise the child, proposing instead that the purity and simplicity of the child's perceptions might operate as a corrective to the distortions of the adult world-view.

Andersen's work has also been an influence upon more recent writers who seek to breach the boundaries between fiction for children and fiction for adults. The first book of Philip Pullman's *His Dark Materials* trilogy, *Northern Lights* (Pullman 1995; *The*

Golden Compass in North America), echoes 'The Snow Queen' in its account of a young girl's redemptive quest to the frozen North to save her companion, and in its philosophical exploration of a conflict between the life-giving human spirit and arid doctrinal rationalism. More generally, writers from C. S. Lewis to Salman Rushdie owe a literary debt to Andersen for pioneering the artistic practice of reimagining the world from both an adult and a child's perceptions simultaneously. Nowhere is this debt better expressed than in the similarity between Andersen's description of his 'new' fairy tales cited above, and Salman Rushdie's description of his allegorical and philosophical novels for children, *Haroun and the Sea of Stories* (1990) and *Luka and the Fire of Life* (2010). 'It has been my aim, in *Luka* as in *Haroun*,' Rushdie observes:

> to write a story that demolishes the boundary between 'adult' and 'children's' literature. One way I have thought about *Luka* and *Haroun* is that each of them is a message in a bottle. A child may read these books and, I hope, derive from them the pleasures and satisfactions that children seek from books. The same child may read them again when he or she is grown, and see a different book, with adult satisfactions instead of (or as well as) the earlier ones.
>
> (Rushdie 2010b)

Whether intentional or not, the intellectual heritage of this statement begins with Andersen.

Much as Andersen has been a vital influence upon the development of literature for children, however, his stories can appear excessively punitive to modern sensibilities. In the story of 'The Little Mermaid', the heroine must endure protracted suffering, including enforced dumbness, before she finally martyrs herself for a selfish prince. In the story of 'The Red Shoes', comparably, the protagonist Karen, because of her desire for a pair of red shoes (which symbolise both vanity and sexuality), is forced to endure a painful redemptive struggle before she finally achieves the ultimate expiation of her sins in death. Writing of the prolonged agony of both these protagonists, the children's writer P. L. Travers accuses Andersen of 'cruelty, sustained, deliberate, contrived', and argues that 'his tortures, disguised as piety, are subtle, often demoralising' (quoted in Tatar 1999: 212). Comparably, Angela Carter, in a tongue-in-cheek response to Andersen's fairy tales written for *New Society* in 1975, reflects on the violence done to women in 'The Red Shoes' and 'The Little Mermaid' and concludes that '[a] sensitive child might come to less emotional harm if he sticks to soft-core porn, rather than Andersen' (Carter 1997: 452). Feminist critics of Andersen's works have also found evidence of misogyny in these elaborate portraits of suffering women, arguing that Andersen demonstrates in them a fear of female sexuality, and a desire to counteract that fear by promoting self-sacrifice and silent suffering as ideals for female behaviour. Andersen's depictions of female characters, however, are never straightforward. In 'The Snow Queen', Gerda, like the Little Mermaid and Karen in 'The Red Shoes', must endure a process of self-sacrifice and ritualistic purification before she is able to redeem her companion Kai, and in this respect she may be seen as another female victim who is asked to give up her agency for the sake of male self-realisation; but her long struggle to rescue Kai also has heroic dimensions, and on her journey she is aided by powerful female figures such as the old Lapp woman and the old Finn woman. This narrative also gives us one of the most potent female characters in the canon of classic fairy tales: the entrancing and ambiguous figure of the Little Robber Girl who rides a reindeer and always sleeps with her knife, but who, unusually in fairy tales, remains unpunished for her agency and her subversive tendencies ('I got a lot of very positive input from the splendid little robber girl,' Carter concedes: she is 'a small image of emancipation'; Carter 1997: 452). The critique of Andersen's attitude to women in his tales also needs to be tempered by the recognition that Andersen, working in the autobiographical mode, often casts himself in the role of his female characters. As Hans Brix proposed early in the twentieth century, 'The Little Mermaid' is a complex allegorical self-portrait of Andersen that is expressive of his feelings of being split between two worlds: between the Odense of his childhood, and the Copenhagen of his later years, and between his working-class origins, and the aristocratic circles in which he came to move (Wullschlager 2001: 167). The mermaid is also, Wullschlager argues, a figuration of his feelings of bisexuality, created at a moment of crisis for Andersen, when Edvard Collin, with whom he had formed an intense attachment, was married to Henriette Thyberg. Edvard, in this reading, is the faithless prince, who is unable or unwilling to recognise the adoration of the mermaid, and so marries another; Andersen is the silent suffering half-half creature, unable to speak his love, but also unable to give it up (Andersen 2004: notes 426). The redemptive suffering that Andersen often enforces upon his female characters, if the stories are read in these terms, is at least in part a portrait of his own suffering, and his inclination to punish and purify is a product of his complex response to his own feelings of ambiguity and uncertainty about sex and sexuality.

By the time Andersen died in 1875, he had transformed the literary fairy tale into a mainstay of children's literature, and created a modern form for the genre: contemporary in setting, direct in style, allegorical in intent. Ever restless as an artist, however, Andersen by this stage was moving beyond the convention he himself had established and exploring new artistic territory. In 1852 he changed the title of his story collections once more to *Historier* (*Stories*), omitting the phrase 'fairy tale' altogether; and finally, from 1855 to the end of his fairy-tale writing career in 1872, he combined the two titles into *Nye Eventyr og Historier* (*New Fairy Tales and Stories*) (see Godden 2004: 36). These last tales comprise Andersen's final phase of story-writing; they are often experimental in conception and in form, and they resist the conventions of linear narrative. His final story, 'Aunty Toothache', for instance, with its disjointed and fragmentary structure, its impressionistic style and surreal imagery, anticipates by some twenty years the experiments with fiction that would be conducted around the turn of the century by a new generation of artists and writers who would reject the certitudes and complacencies of nineteenth-century literature, and begin to create a fiction for a more uncertain time. The following passage, in which toothache becomes personified, is indicative:

> On the floor sat a figure, tall and thin, the kind a child draws with a pencil on a slate, something that is supposed to look like a person. A single thin line forms the body, one line and then another form the arms; the legs are each one line, the head a polygon.

Soon the figure grew more distinct. It was wearing a sort of gown, very thin, very fine, but this showed that the figure was female.

I heard a buzzing. Was it her or the wind that was droning like a botfly through the crack in the pane?

No, it was her, Madame Toothache! Her Horrible Highness, *Satania infernalis*. God save us from her visits!

'How nice it is to be here,' she hummed. 'Such nice quarters. Marshy ground, boggy ground. The mosquitoes have buzzed around here with poison in their stingers. Now I have the stinger, and it has to be sharpened on human teeth. They're shining so white in this fellow in the bed. They've braved sweet and sour, hot and cold, nut-shells and plum pits. But I'll smack them and whack them, I'll mulch the roots with a drafty gust and give them cold feet.'

What a horrible speech, what a horrible guest!

'Oh, so you're a poet,' she said. 'Well, I'm going to write you into all the verses of pain. I'm going to give you iron and steel in your body, put fibre into all the fibres of your nerves.'

It felt as if a glowing awl were passing through my cheekbone. I twisted and writhed.

(Andersen 2004: 418–19)

Not without reason does Angela Carter claim that '[t]hose Arthur Rackham illustrations to Anderson [*sic*] are all wrong' and that 'Munch would have been far more suitable' (Carter 1997: 451). The passage above not only anticipates Edvard Munch's painting *The Scream* (1893) with its stark depiction of human suffering; it also anticipates the lean and disorientating style of the Expressionist movement more generally. Thus Andersen, in his final work, strikes the death blow to the upholstered prettiness of the nineteenth-century fairy tale and, in so doing, ushers into the era of experimental modernity a genre that had been imagined by the Grimms to be forever backward looking.

4

THE EMERGENCE OF FAIRY-TALE THEORY
PLATO TO PROPP

BEFORE GRIMM

Folk-narrative studies as an academic discipline is generally supposed to have begun with the prefaces, essays and notes that accompany the *Kinder- und Hausmärchen* of the Brothers Grimm. Though the Grimms pioneered a scientific folklore, however, they were by no means the first to reflect speculatively upon that curious mass of traditional narrative materials that have been assembled under the titles, variously, of 'old wives' tales', 'popular remains', 'tales of mother goose' and 'fairy tales'. Amongst the earliest surviving comments on popular narrative traditions are those found in Plato's *Gorgias* (c. 380 BCE) and *Republic* (c. 360 BCE), in which various forms of *mythos* (story) are mentioned, including, notably, the *mythos graos* – old woman's tale (Warner 1995: 14). According to Plato, however, the philosopher Socrates did not have much that is complimentary to say about these fictions. In the *Gorgias*, Socrates observes that old women's tales are fictions which a rational man ought properly to despise (Plato 1925: 527a4); and in *The Republic* he bans any 'casual tales which may be devised by casual persons' from the education of the future guardians of his ideal republic on the basis that they infect impressionable minds with false beliefs and immoral ideas (Plato 1953: 377b–378e).

Comparable attitudes to popular tradition resurface periodically in European culture. In the sixteenth and seventeenth centuries humanist scholars repeatedly disparaged popular tales as superstitious nonsense disseminated by 'aged mumping beldames' (Thomas Nashe, quoted in Lamb 2006: 45), and urged that the young should be exposed only to elevated reading matter from the classics and from history (see Lamb 2006: 45–62). Hence in 1529, in *De pueris instituendis* (*On Education for Children*), Erasmus, as the most influential scholar of his age, recommended that the young should be encouraged to learn 'a pretty story from the ancient poets, or a memorable tale from history' in place of 'the old wives' fairy rubbish such as most children are steeped in nowadays by nurses and serving women' (cited in Lamb 2006: 53). Half a century later, the classicist William Lowth can be found directly endorsing Plato's instruction to 'Nurses' in his translation of Battus's *De Oeconomia Christiania* (1581):

> *Plato* seemeth verie diligently to admonish Nurses that they sing not to their babes and yong infantes everie trifling tale, rusticke ryme, baudie Ballet, and olde wives fabled fantasies, lest from their cradles it shall fortune, that they be nouseled in folly, and frought with corrupt conditions, and too bolde behaviour.
>
> (Cited in Lamb 2006: 51)

In such observations, as Mary Ellen Lamb argues, sixteenth-century male scholars performed a rejection of the cultures of their early childhood, associated with femininity and close contact with the lower classes, and sought instead to assert their identification with classical modes of learning, coded as masculine and elite (Lamb 2006: 51–54).

In the late seventeenth and eighteenth centuries, too, the Socratic objection to storytelling combines with philosophical rationalism to produce a potent brew of intellectual and moral objections to popular tales. The English philosopher John Locke, shortly before the turn of the seventeenth century in *Some Thoughts Concerning Education* (1693), argued influentially that 'impressions and notions of *spirits* and *goblins*' delivered to the young through 'the indiscretion of servants' were damaging to the mind (Richardson 2009: 35). Strongly influenced by such philosophical objections to popular traditions, writers of improving children's literature of the later eighteenth and early nineteenth century sought to replace the fairy tales that were becoming popular in chapbook publications with instructional tales designed to affirm the virtues of the day and punish its vices. Reigning supreme in this moralistic pantheon were figures such as Little Goody Two-Shoes (*The History of Little Goody Two-Shoes*, John Newberry, 1765) and Primrose Prettyface (*The Renowned History of Primrose Prettyface*, 1785): both of whom are upstanding Cinderellas who manage to elevate themselves from rags to riches not by the force of magic, but by '*Sweetness of Temper and Love of Learning*' (Richardson 2009: 38–39). By contrast, 'Mother Bunch' and her 'Fairy Tales' were judged, by moralising educationalists such as 'The Guardian of Education' Mrs Trimmer, to be 'only fit to fill the heads of children with confused notions of wonderland and supernatural events, brought about by the agency of imaginary beings' (Richardson 2009: 35; see also Pickering 1981: 40–69).

In this atmosphere of profound mistrust of traditional tales, it is hardly surprising that a rigorous fairy-tale scholarship fails to develop. For most commentators, from the classical period to the Enlightenment, fairy tales were foolish fictions, not worth serious consideration, and certainly beneath the notice of educated men. One notable exception to this rule is the antiquarian scholar John Aubrey (1626–97) who, though writing in the era of John Locke's philosophical ascendancy, was prepared to reflect fondly upon 'old women and mayds' who told 'fabulous stories nightimes, of Sprights and walking of Ghosts' (Lamb 2006: 47), and to lament the possible loss of these fictions, which he believed were being 'putt ... out of doors' by technical advancements in printing, an increase in literacy, and social disruptions caused by the English Civil War (Dorson 1968: 5–6). Even Aubrey, however, when he comes to reflect upon the significance and value of 'old wives tales' at the start of his *Remaines of Gentilisme and Judaisme* (ms. 1688, pub. 1881), is hesitant and apologetic. 'Old Customs and old wives fables are grosse things,' he writes:

> [B]ut yet ought not to be buried in Oblivion; there may some trueth and usefulnesse be picked out of them, besides tis' a pleasure to consider the Errours that enveloped former ages: as also the present.
>
> (Quoted in Dorson 1968: 7)

Before the second half of the eighteenth century, this is perhaps as close as any writer comes to defending the fairy tale as a legitimate object of scholarly interest.

With the dawning of the era of European Romanticism, however, comes a distinct shift in attitude. In Britain, the poets Samuel Taylor Coleridge, William Wordsworth and Charles Lamb began to challenge the primacy of instructional literature for children, and to argue that imaginative literature without an explicit morality might have more value as a means of opening the mind to higher truths. In a letter to Thomas Poole dated 16 October 1797, Coleridge writes that he knows of 'no other way of giving the mind a love of "the Great", and "the Whole"' than through the reading, in childhood, of fairy tales and romances (quoted in Watson 2009: 24). Charles Lamb, in an 1802 letter to Coleridge about the reading habits of Coleridge's son Hartley, is more forthright in his condemnation of the narrowness of improving literature for children by writers such as Mrs Barbauld, and instead celebrates the impact upon the imagination of 'wild tales' of unbridled fancy:

> Knowledge insignificant and vapid as Mrs. B[arbauld]'s books convey ... must come to a child in the *shape of knowledge*, and his empty noddle must be turned with conceit of his own powers when he has learned that a Horse is an animal, and Billy is better than a Horse, and such like; instead of that beautiful interest in wild tales which made the child a man, while all the time he suspected himself to be no bigger than a child. ... Think what you would have been now, if instead of being fed with Tales and old wives' fables in childhood, you had been crammed with geography and natural history?
>
> (Quoted in Watson 2009: 25)

Coleridge and Wordsworth had also, in their influential preface to the second edition of the *Lyrical Ballads* (1800), challenged the idea that the attitudes and perceptions of the common people were culturally and artistically inferior, asserting instead that the common people, especially when in rural environments, had an immediacy of perception, a natural responsiveness, that enabled them to speak more truthfully about the world than highly educated and civilised men schooled in the artificialities of rhetoric (Wordsworth 1994: 433–34). Simultaneously, in Germany, intellectuals associated with the Romantic Nationalist movement, including J. G. W. Herder, Ludwig Tieck and Friedrich Schlegel, were redefining folk songs as the fragmentary remains of the *naturepoesie* (natural poetry) of antique nations, and presenting the 'folk' as guardians of an ancestral heritage. So influential were these ideas that, within a generation, the image of the foolish, superstitious old woman peddling dangerous lies had ceased to be so dominant, and had been replaced by an equally potent mythology: the image of the homely, kind and truthful carrier of ancient wisdoms, whose stories had the power to remind nations of their antique roots. Neither of these mythologies offers a credible account of how folk narratives originate and what their significances might be: the Romantic myth of the folk narrative, that presents it as a pure emanation of nature, is just as misleading as the rationalist attitude that dismisses it as absurd superstition. In the new seriousness that Romanticism granted the folk and fairy tale, however, lay the cultural licence for the evolution of a folk-narrative scholarship; and it was in this fertile intellectual soil that the Grimms began collecting and writing about popular narrative traditions.

THE SUN FROG: NINETEENTH-CENTURY FOLKLORISTICS

The first narrative to appear in the Grimm collection is 'Der Froschkönig oder der eiserne Heinrich' (1812; 'The Frog King, or Iron Heinrich'), a German version of the tale type ATU440 supplied to the Grimms by members of the Wild family, and reworked by the Grimms in successive editions of the *Kinder- und Hausmärchen*. The Grimm story concerns a princess who accidentally drops her golden ball in a well and makes a rash agreement with a frog that, if it will swim down to the bottom of the well and fetch the ball, she will allow it to become her 'companion and playmate', permitted to sit beside her at table, eat from her golden plate, drink from her cup and sleep in her bed (Grimm and Grimm 1992: 2). The princess hardly expects the frog to hold her to the bargain, but of course, the frog appears the following day to claim its reward. At first the princess tries to renege on her promise, but the princess's father forces her to fulfil her obligations to the creature, and so she lets it eat from her plate and drink from her cup. When finally the frog asks the princess to be put into her bed, however, she becomes angry and throws it against the wall. This act of sudden and strange violence brings about the resolution of the tale: the frog turns into a king, the king reveals that he was under a spell and the princess marries the metamorphosed frog king 'in keeping with her father's wishes' (Grimm and Grimm 1992: 4). The story then concludes with a brief digression concerning the Frog King's loyal servant, Heinrich, who has bands of sorrow wrapped around his heart which burst when his master is released from the spell.

In their notes to 'The Frog King' the Grimms give outlines of several parallel versions of the story: one from Hesse, one from Paderborn and one from Scotland, where it was recorded in 1549 in the *Complaynt of Scotland* (Hunt 1884: I, 339). In the Scottish version, there is no father to enforce the moral lesson (keep your promises!), and the obligation to the frog does not come about because of a golden ball, but because a lady is sent by her stepmother to draw water from the well of the world's end. The Grimms summarise the remainder of the story as follows:

> She arrives at the well, after encountering many dangers, but soon perceives that her adventures have not come to a conclusion. A frog emerges from the well, and before it suffers her to draw water, obliges her to betroth herself to the monster, under penalty of being torn to pieces. The lady returns safe, but at midnight the frog-lover appears at the door and demands entrance, according to promise, to the great consternation of the lady and her nurse.

'Open the door, my hinny, my hart,
Open the door, my ain wee thing;
And mind the words that you and I spak,
Down in the meadow at the well-spring.'

The frog is admitted, and addresses her:

'Take me up on your knee, my dearie,
Take me up on your knee, my dearie,
And mind the words that you and I spak
At the cauld well sae weary.'

The frog is finally disenchanted, and appears in his original
form as a prince.

(Hunt 1884: I, 340)

Comparative data of this kind, which appears in the notes for
most of the Grimms' tales, plays an important methodological role
in the collection, and constitutes one of the major contributions of
the Grimms to the nineteenth-century understanding of the nature
of folk narrative: it demonstrates that popular fictions such as 'The
Frog King' existed in multiple international variants, and that these
international variants exhibit both continuities, which make it possible to identify stories as fictions of a similar type, and differences,
which mark them off as variant performances of the same core narrative. This kind of narrative information, furthermore, which was
elaborated and extended by folklorists and anthropologists
throughout the nineteenth century, brought into focus a set of
questions which were to characterise scholarly enquiry into folk-
narrative traditions from the 1800s onwards. Folklorists began to
ask: how did it come about that these narratives could be found in so
many different places in so many different forms? Had they originated in one place and spread? Or had similar narratives been
invented independently of each other? And what factors could
explain the variations between tales of the same type? Were variations
a product of adaptation over time? Or could some other explanation be offered for differences between narratives of similar types?

Three broad hypotheses were developed in the nineteenth century
in response to these questions: the hypothesis of an antique

mythical origin for popular European traditions, the theory that folk narratives were 'survivals' from the primitive stages of civilisation, and the theory that all folk narratives had originated in India and then spread as a result of human migration. The mythical theory was favoured by the Grimms, and remained dominant for the first part of the nineteenth century. It held that European *märchen* were the degenerate remains of a grand mythology belonging to the ancestors of Indo-European peoples, and had come into being after these ancestors (the 'Aryans') had dispersed throughout the Indo-European area between the third and fourth millennia BCE, scattering narrative fragments like seeds as they went. These narrative fragments, according to the hypothesis, had taken diverse roots, and in the course of time a host of different tale versions had grown up, varied in detail, nurtured by new soils, but all linked distantly to a single Aryan ur-mythology. The Grimms evoke this idea eloquently in the critical materials accompanying the second edition of the tales when they propose that surviving German *märchen* contain a 'mythic element' that is like 'small pieces of a shattered jewel ... lying strewn on a ground all overgrown with grass and flowers' (Hunt 1884: II, 579–80). If this mythic element were to be traced back to 'the outermost lines of common property', they speculate, it would be found to be 'coterminous with [the myths] of the great race which is commonly called Indo-Germanic' (Hunt 1884: II, 580). A similar idea is also invoked by the Grimms in the preface to the first volume of the *Kinder- und Hausmärchen*, though here they swap their mineralogical metaphor for a vegetable one: German *märchen*, they claim, are like the scattered remains of a once-mighty crop of ancient Germanic folk poetry, blasted by the storms of modernity and change but surviving nonetheless in the 'places by the stove, the hearth in the kitchen, attic stairs, holidays still celebrated, meadows and forests in their solitude, and above all the untrammelled imagination' (Tatar 2003: 252–53). Two compelling ideas follow from this hypothesis of Aryan origin. The first is that any attempt to reassemble the scattered stories constitutes an endeavour to recover something of this foundational Aryan mythology, to reform the shattered jewel, or reseed the mighty crop. This idea lends powerful support to the nationalist objective of nineteenth-century

folkloristics, since it allows folklore collectors to claim that in assembling the traditional materials of a nation or ethnic group they are contributing to the recovery of a grand narrative of cultural foundation. In the following century, this idea also became a mainstay of fascist folkloristics, in which context it became part of an ideological programme to forge the image of an ethnically pure root civilisation for Germanic peoples that would support the identification of a master race destined by blood-right to rule. Such uses of their ideas could not, of course, have been anticipated or endorsed by the Grimms, who were passionate about preserving elements of an embattled German culture, but remained humanists and internationalists in outlook. Nevertheless, the use of folk traditions to reinforce an idea of ancestral national belonging, and the idea that the tales of the present should be used to bolster a mythology of a strong past that could yet be recovered, has, since the 1930s and 1940s, become resonant of fascism, and some scholars, retrospectively, have criticised the Grimms for nurturing this kind of nationalist feeling in their collection (see Wilson 1973; Snyder 1978; and Ellis 1983).

The second influential idea to follow from the Aryan hypothesis was that modern European *märchen* would be better understood if more could be learned about the Aryan civilisations from which the stories were said to have descended. This latter line of thought was pursued most influentially by the German philologist and Sanskritist Max Müller (1823–1900), born in Dessau but resident in England from 1846. Through a comparative analysis of ancient Indo-European languages such as Greek, Latin and Sanskrit, each of which was argued to have originated in the forgotten source language of the Aryans, Müller claimed that he had been able to make certain deductions about the character of Aryan peoples. The Aryans, he alleged, were a people of 'healthy and strong feelings', who had 'a nicely organised family life' that they used as a basis for peaceable government (Müller 1872: 127 and 38–41); they were also sun worshippers, and expressed their sun worship in poetical ways, devising complex 'mythopoetic' metaphors to describe the sun and its movements through the heavens. It was these metaphors of solar transit, Müller speculated, that were the basis of myths and stories deriving from the Aryan civilisation.

To fully understand the original meanings of these stories, there-fore, we need only reinvest them with the metaphorical meanings which time and forgetfulness have stripped out of them. This assumption forms the basis of Müller's interpretation of the story of the Frog King. The ancient Sanskrit Vedas, according to Müller, show that one of the ancient mythopoetic names for the sun was 'Bhekî', the female form of 'frog', and this came about because 'at sunrise and sunset', the sun looks like a frog 'squatting on the water' (Müller 1872: 245). In Aryan speech, accordingly, the conflation between sun and frog was incorporated into certain sayings and stories designed to express the passage of the sun across the sky, rising from the sea at dawn like a frog emerging from the water and setting in the sea at evening like a frog diving back into the depths. Initially, the metaphorical character of these expressions was fully understood by our ancestors. In the long course of millennia, however, as these sayings and stories were handed down from generation to generation, their original meta-phorical meanings were forgotten or distorted, and the association between frog and sun broken. All that remains to the present, therefore, is a set of stories about anthropomorphic frogs, with no trace of the original sun myths they derived from. Stories of this kind, Müller insists, are 'absurd' – '[n]o poet could ever have sat down to invent sheer nonsense like this'; but happily for the dignity of our ancient ancestors it is possible, using Müller's techniques of analysis, to retrace the story to a more rational set of meanings (Müller 1872: 245). Understood for the metaphor that it originally was, the story of the frog that climbs out of a well and marries a princess resolves itself into a logical account of solar transit: the frog, rising from the well at the start of the story, signifies the sun rising out of the water at morning, and the transformation of the frog into a prince at the end of the story signifies the sun's disappearance at night (Müller 1872: 245–46).

Müller's theories aroused widespread interest when they were first espoused in the 1860s and 1870s. To an equal extent, however, they invited challenges, notably from the Scottish anthropological folklorist Andrew Lang (1844–1912), who protested, in a series of publications from 1873 ('Mythology and Fairy Tales' in *The Fort-nightly Review*) to 1897 (*Modern Mythology: A Reply to Max Müller*), that Müller, and disciples of Müller such as Sir George Cox, had created a misleading, and indeed highly fanciful, idea of the character and meaning of myths and folk narratives. Four particular objections are adduced by Lang in his introduction to Margaret Hunt's translation of *Grimm's Household Tales* (1884): first, that the philological method relies upon unfounded and unprovable speculation about the original meanings of Sanskrit words; second, that philologists differ amongst themselves about the possible original meanings of these words, thus demonstrating the unreliability of the method; third, that philological interpretation often depends upon character names that have been added to the stories at a later date; and fourth, that nature myths, when they are genuine nature myths, generally advertise themselves as such, and there is no intelligible reason why it should be necessary or logical to identify all myths, all romances, all epics, all folk tales as 'nature-myths in disguise' (Lang 1884b: xxxii). For these reasons Lang is especially scornful of Müller's theory about the Sun Frog:

> In old times (Mr. Müller says) the sun had many names. 'It can be shown that "frog" was an ancient name for the sun.' But though it can be shown, Mr. Müller never shows it. He observes 'this feminine Bheki (frog) must at one time have been used as a name for the sun.' But though he himself asks for 'chapter and verse from the [Rig] Veda', he gives us no verse and no chapter for his assertions.
>
> (Lang 1884b: xxxvii)

In place of Müller's tenuous speculation, therefore, Lang advances his own hypothesis that folk tales derive, not from the myths of an ancient civilisation, but from primitive tribes who told magical stories in reflection of their own magical world-views. In primitive societies, Lang argues, savage customs and savage beliefs predominate: there is endemic credulity in 'magic and sorcery', a 'common faith in friendly or protecting animals', and 'strong ideas about the persistent existence of the souls of the dead' (Lang 1913: 48–51); these customs and beliefs, furthermore, are reflected in the stories that primitive peoples tell in which magic is not only possible but unremarkable, and in which animals talk and the dead return. As society develops, Lang proposes, such primitive ideas cease to be seriously entertained and so become obsolete; but traces of savage thought remain in myths and folk tales to remind civilised societies that they have 'passed through a condition quite unlike that of civilised man – a condition in which things seem natural and rational that now appear devoid of reason' (Lang 1913: 32). Folklore, in Lang's view, thus represents 'in the midst of a civilised race, the savage ideas out of which civilisation has been evolved,' and the folklorist, when confronted with 'the fact which puzzles ... by its presence in civilisation' should usually conclude that it 'is a relic surviving from the time when the ancestors of a civilised race were in a state of savagery' (Lang 1884a: 25). Lang's own interpretation of the 'Frog King' narrative thus runs as follows:

> To the savage intellect, man and beast are on a level, and all savage myth makes men descended from beasts; while stories of the loves of gods in bestial shape, or the unions of men and animals, incessantly occur. 'Unnatural' as these notions seem to us, no ideas are more familiar to savages, and none recur more frequently in Indo-Aryan, Scandinavian, and Greek mythology. An extant tribe in North-West America still claims descent from a frog. The wedding of Bheki and the king is a survival, in Sanskrit, of a tale of this kind.
>
> (Lang 1884a: 79)

It is in this way, Lang further argues, that we may explain the common appearance of such elements in folk tales and myths all over the world, for if there are similarities in 'the savage mind everywhere and in all races', then it follows logically that different races around the globe will develop similar stories that articulate these 'similar mental habits and ideas' (Lang 1913: 41). Lang thus rejects arguments that depend upon gradual dissemination from a single source to explain the commonality of certain kinds of fiction in diverse societies, and instead advances an argument for 'independent invention'. Lang also maintains, however, that whilst diverse societies may invent comparable story elements independently, it is improbable that they will independently develop entire complex *plots*. '[T]he diffusion of similar incidents in countries widely severed,' he writes:

> may be ... ascribed to the identical beliefs of early man all over the
> world. But the diffusion of plots is much more hard to explain, nor do
> we venture to explain it, except by the chances of transmission in the
> long past of human existence.
>
> (Lang 1884b: lxx)

Thus whilst simple story motifs are likely to be subject to polygenesis (multiple origins), complex tale types are more likely to have come into being in a single place (monogenesis) and then spread through human migratory dissemination. Lang's argument, therefore, involves a fluid mix of independent invention and dissemination.

Different as they are in the conclusions that they draw, the arguments of Lang and Müller have one thing in common: they both locate the meaning and the significance of the folk tale in the past. For Müller, these narratives have no meaning for modern-day readers (they are 'absurd'), but remain worthy of a scholar's attention because they tell us how our ancestors saw the world six millennia ago. For Lang, likewise, these stories, so far as civilised peoples are concerned, are essentially obsolete in their significance: they represent a mode of thinking and acting that civilisation has left behind. A contemporary analysis of fairy tales is likely to come to very different conclusions. For the modern reader, 'The Frog King' does not appear to be a narrative that is useful only as a means of comprehending a past that has been superseded; quite the contrary, it seems to be a narrative that speaks meaningfully to the present. It also appears to modern readers as a narrative that is shaped by social and cultural designs that are of a more recent vintage than dim antiquity: the patriarchal arrangement, in which a girl is handed to a suitor under the supervision of her father, for instance, belongs as much to early-nineteenth-century Germany as it does to the savage marriage rites of forgotten eras.

This paradigmatic shift, from reading the fairy tale as a narrative that is essentially of the past to reading it as a narrative that speaks meaningfully to the present, is motivated by several developments. In part, it is caused by changing attitudes to the folklore text that allow us to regard the folk tale as a narrative form that is ceaselessly refigured and reframed by the new contexts into which it is absorbed. In part too it is a result of the rejection by anthropologists and folklorists of the paternalistic distinction made by Lang between modern post-Enlightenment European 'civilisation', which does not believe in magic and so only acknowledges fairy tales as toys, and 'savage' or 'primitive' societies that accept folk magic as part of their reality. Above all, however, this shift in attitudes to fairy tale is a result of the revolution in thought precipitated by Sigmund Freud that was under way before both Lang and Müller were in their graves, and that, had they known about it, would have posed some serious challenges to their assumptions about the folk tale. The extent of this revolution in thought becomes apparent if we compare the explanations given by Müller and Lang for the irrational elements to be found in fairy tales with the explanation given by Freud. For Müller, the irrational in fairy tale can be rationalised by reference to ancient solar beliefs because solar mythology makes it possible to redescribe all irrational elements in fairy tales as metaphors for natural phenomena. For Lang, alternatively, fabulous elements in fairy tale represent a form of thought that has been superseded and abandoned in the course of civilisation's advancement. For Freud, however, the irrational in the folk tale can only be explained by reference to repressed anxieties and desires that remain a persistant part of human psychic experience, and that have to be continually suppressed in the interests of civili-sation. Freud thus punctures Victorian complacency about its own supreme rationality: these are not states of mind that we have left behind, he proposes, but states of mind that we have repressed. In so arguing, he presents the fairy tale in an entirely new light: as a form of fiction that speaks, not only of the mentality of antiquity, but also of the latent underside of the present.

THE HISTORIC-GEOGRAPHIC METHOD AND THE CLASSIFICATION OF *MÄRCHEN*

For late Victorians such as Lang, lack of concrete documentary evidence, combined with the vast time-scales under investigation, rendered the problem of discovering the complete life history of a particular story insuperable: 'We only know for certain,' he wrote in his introduction to the *contes* of Perrault, 'that there is practically no limit to the chances of transmission in the remote past of the race':

> Wherever man, woman, or child can go, there a tale may go, and may find a new home. Any drifted and wandering canoe, any captured alien wife, any stolen slave passed from hand to hand in commerce or war, may carry a *Märchen*. These processes of transmission have been going on, practically, ever since man was man. Thus it is even more difficult to limit the possibilities of transmission than the chances of coincidence. But the chances of coincidence also are numerous. The *ideas* and *situations* of popular tales are all afloat, everywhere, in the imaginations of early and of pre-scientific men. Who can tell how often they might casually unite in similar wholes, independently combined?
> (Lang 1888: cxv)

Such was the prevailing attitude in 1888. In the early twentieth century, however, the Finnish scholars Kaarle Krohn (1863–1933) and Antti Aarne (1867–1925) proposed a theory about narrative transmission that they believed would enable folklorists to make scientifically based reconstructions of the genealogy of any particular story, provided sufficient data about that story could be accurately collected. Central to this theory was the idea that a specific tale type originates in one place, and is then disseminated, and adapted by individual tellers as it spreads. Operating on this assumption, they argued that it should be possible to recompose the history of any given narrative by collecting all the available variations of a particular story, plotting when and where those variants had been recorded, determining at which points particular changes had been introduced into the narrative, and, by that means, retracing the journey of the story from the outer regions it had reached, to the source from which it came. The story discovered at the outer limits they argued would be the most corrupt (more innovations and additions would have been made); the story at the centre from which it had originally spread would be the most pure, and would thus give an indication of what the tale type looks like in its essential form (Thompson 1977: 430). Seminal applications of this method, known as the 'historic-geographic' method, include Stith Thompson's analysis of the American Indian 'Star Husband Tale' (Thompson 1952) and Warren E. Roberts's extensive account of the 'Kind and Unkind Girls' tale type (1958 [Roberts 1995]). The method also gave rise to the composition of a series of indexes, designed to support investigations into the historic and geographic spread of tale types. These included, most importantly, Aarne's *Das Verzeichnis der Märchentypen* in 1910, translated and revised by Stith Thompson in 1928 as *The Types of the Folktale* (second revision, 1961), and the motif index compiled by Thompson between 1932 and 1936 (revised and enlarged, 1955–58). More recently, the German scholar Hans-Jörg Uther has also issued a revised version of the Aarne/Thompson tale-type index under the title *The Types of International Folktales: A Classification and Bibliography* (Uther 2004). In this revision Uther and his team of scholars have endeavoured to address some of the criticisms made in the intervening years of the Aarne/Thompson system. In response to the charge that tale-type descriptions in *The Types of the Folktale* express gender bias, the descriptions of tales have been extensively rewritten. The range of tale types indexed has also been expanded significantly in order to make the index genuinely international rather than broadly Indo-European with an arbitrary scattering of tale types from other regions (Uther 2004: 7–12). Even in Uther's hands, however, the system remains vulnerable to one of the cardinal charges levelled against it by its critics: that the descriptions of tale types are inconsistent because they depend upon narrative contents that are variable, rather than elements of narrative structure that are constant (Dundes 2007: 101–5).

This confusion in the Aarne system of indexing was first highlighted by the Russian formalist, Vladimir Propp, in the introduction to his *Morfológija skázki*, published in 1928 and translated into English by Laurence Scott as *Morphology of the Folktale* in 1958 (second edition 1968). Observing that Aarne, in the first edition of the Index, divides fairy tales between the categories of (1) a supernatural adversity; (2) a supernatural husband or wife; (3) a supernatural task; (4) a supernatural helper; (5) a magic object; (6) supernatural power or knowledge; and (7) any other supernatural element, Propp asks what is to be done, so far as classification is concerned, with 'those tales in which a supernatural task is resolved by a supernatural helper (which occurs very often), or those in which a supernatural spouse is also a supernatural helper' (Propp 1968: 10). Clearly, tales exist that might be put into two or more categories – and if this is the case, then Aarne's system of classification cannot be regarded as one that makes logical or objective distinctions between species of fairy tale. 'If types do exist,' Propp concludes, 'they exist not on the level indicated by Aarne, but on the level of the structural features of similar tales' (11).

The importance of this observation for folk- and fairy-tale studies, and indeed for literary theory more generally, cannot be underestimated. It is the starting point of Propp's own theory of the folk tale, in which he argues that distinctions between tale types need to be made at the level of form rather than at the level of contents. It is also one of the starting points of formalist and structuralist approaches to literature more generally.

VLADIMIR PROPP AND THE MORPHOLOGY OF FAIRY TALE

Propp's morphological analysis of fairy tales begins with the observation that, though the range of incident in fairy tales is very broad, though its command of the fabulous image is kaleidoscopic, the patterns that appear in the plots of fairy tales are strikingly regular. The same kinds of thing happen again and again; and there is, what is more, a remarkable consistency with which incident follows incident. Propp was the first scholar to offer a comprehensive description of this phenomenon. Fairy tales, he suggested, appear superficially diverse because certain kinds of incident that occur in the narratives may be realised in a dizzying variety of ways; but underlying this diversity of realisation is a remarkable consistency in the functions that each incident will fulfil in the plot of a fairy tale. Thus, though the complexions an event might take in a tale are abundant, the form of the event will remain stable and predictable.

To illustrate this, Propp lists four events that occur near to the start of four different stories from the prominent Russian collection of tales *Rússkie naródnye skázki (Russian Folktales)* made by Aleksander Afanás'ev between 1855 and 1864:

1   A tsar gives an eagle to a hero. The eagle carries the hero away to another kingdom.

2   An old man gives Súčenko a horse. The horse carries Súčenko away to another kingdom.

3   A sorcerer gives Iván a little boat. The boat takes Iván to another kingdom.

4   A princess gives Iván a ring. Young men appearing from out of the ring carry Iván away into another kingdom.

(Propp 1968: 19–20)

Clearly there are two ways of looking at these occurrences. In the individual tale, for the sake of the colour and the life of that tale, these are different events belonging to different stories. In their underlying pattern, however, they are the same kinds of events belonging to the same basic structure. In every case, the hero is in receipt of an item, and in all cases the item transports him to another kingdom. 'Both constants and variables are present,' as Propp notes: 'The names of the dramatis personae change (as well as the attributes of each), but neither their actions nor functions change' (20). If we were to look at a sufficiently large body of fairy tales, Propp proposes, we would find this to be true of every incident of structural importance that occurs in the plot of the fairy tale. In each case, incidents will be realised with pyrotechnic diversity, but in each case it will also be possible to identify these incidents as one of a set of basic structural functions which 'serve as stable, constant elements in a tale, independent of how and by whom they are fulfilled' (21).

Through close analysis of one hundred tales in Afanás'ev's collection, Propp proceeds to identify 31 functions that, he claims, will underlie the structure of every tale. These functions begin with I, ONE OF THE MEMBERS OF A FAMILY ABSENTS HIMSELF FROM HOME, proceed through such developments as XII, THE HERO IS TESTED, and XIV, THE HERO ACQUIRES THE USE OF A MAGICAL AGENT, and conclude with XXX, THE VILLAIN IS PUNISHED, and XXXI, THE HERO IS MARRIED AND ASCENDS THE THRONE. Not all of these functions will appear in every tale, but every tale will be built from a selection of them. These functions, moreover, will, according to Propp, always occur in the sequence in which he has placed them, even when there are intervening functions that are missing ('the absence of certain functions,' Propp explains, 'does not change the order of the rest'; Propp 1968: 22). The implication of this, Propp goes on to demonstrate, is that fairy tales, for all their hyper-abundant richness of incident, are, at an underlying, structural level, based upon the same limited sequence of functions that follow each other in strict order. Thus, as Propp famously and controversially contends: '*All fairy tales are of one type in regard to their structure*' (23): all of them move from the group of functions that involve villainy or the introduction of a 'lack', through the 'intermediary functions' IX to XVIII which involve the tests and trials of the hero, towards the functions XVIII to XXXI: the 'liquidation of lack', the defeat of the villain and the marriage of the hero (92). Propp in this respect anticipates Todorov, who argues that the basic unit of a plot consists of the passage from one equilibrium to another; he also significantly influenced Alan Dundes who, in his analysis of Native American tales, argues that folk narratives typically progress from 'lack' to 'liquidation of lack' (Rosenberg 1991: 98).

The analysis of 'functions' in the *Morphology* is the main business of chapter III, and in the remainder of the book Propp offers a series of qualifications and elaborations. For example, he identifies 'auxilary elements' in tales that are not functions but that serve to connect one function with another; and he demonstrates how sequences of functions can be multiplied to produce the 'trebling' that is so familiar to readers of European fairy tales. The most valuable extension of his argument for the student of folk and fairy tale, however, comes in chapter VI, 'The Distribution of Functions Among the Dramatis Personae', in which Propp argues that the functions of a tale will 'logically join together into certain spheres ... [that] correspond to their respective performers' (Propp 1968: 79). These are the 'spheres of action', of which Propp identifies seven: the sphere of action of the villain, the donor, the helper, the princess, the dispatcher, the hero, and the false hero (79–80). The donor, in this schema, is the figure that provides the hero with magical agents or advice; the dispatcher sends the hero out on a quest; the villain engages in some form of struggle with the hero; the helper renders assistance to the hero; the princess functions as a sought-for-person and may also assign tasks; the false hero temporarily takes the place of the true hero; and the hero is defined by Propp as:

> that character who either directly suffers from the action of the villain in the complication (the one who senses some kind of lack), or who agrees to liquidate the misfortune or lack of another person.
>
> (Propp 1968: 50)

As was the case with the narrative functions, not all these spheres of action need be enacted in every tale. A particular story may not have a false hero or a donor, for instance. Every action that occurs in a fairy tale, however, will, according to Propp, come within the ambit of one of the above spheres. Importantly, these spheres of action do not always coincide exactly with a single character in a tale. It is possible that two different characters will fulfil the plot functions that Propp associates with villainy. For instance, in many versions of 'Cinderella' both the stepsisters of Cinderella and the stepmother operate in the sphere of action of the villain. Conversely, it is possible for a single character in a tale to fulfil functions in two different spheres of action. In the story of 'Rumpelstiltskin', for instance, the figure of Rumpelstiltskin fulfils both the functions associated with the helper ('the solution of difficult tasks') and the functions associated with the villain ('the villain attempts to deceive his victim in order to take possession of him or his belongings'). What matters, in each case, is not the character involved, but the ways in which the actions of a character function within the plot. Propp thus demonstrates the following revolutionary formal and structural principles: (1) that story develops not because of *who performs* but because of *what action* is performed in the development of the plot as a whole, and (2) that the activities of a character depend, not upon the personality of the actor, or their motivations or idiosyncrasies, but on the structural roles they fulfil within the narrative. In Fredric Jameson's terms, Propp has, or at least has sought to, *de-anthropomorphise* narrative studies: to detach it from its concern with the personality of protagonists, and in so doing to displace 'the emphasis that an older, more representational narrative theory put on character' (Jameson 2002: 109–10).

Propp's systematic analysis of the form of the Russian *märchen* has been extremely influential in folk-narrative studies, but it has also been subject to some persuasive scholarly critiques. A principal objection to Propp's model is that not all of his 'functions' and 'spheres of action' are as content-free as his methodology supposes. In the above list of spheres of action, for instance, it is surprising to see a 'princess' specified as the 'sought-for person' in sphere 4. According to the logic of his system, spheres of action should not depend upon variable features of narrative contents such as princesses, but should be capable of being fulfilled by any character of any gender. And yet here, at the centre of this supposedly abstract formal scheme, a princess appears as the ghost of content reinterpreted as form. Propp, we might speculate, makes this apparent error for two reasons. The first is methodological: when he constructs his **morphology** he consults *only narratives with male protagonists*, and so inevitably produces a system that analyses the structure of tales with male protagonists. The second is ideological: Propp is operating from within a patriarchal paradigm that inclines him to see culturally specific models of gendered behaviour (active prince, passive princess) as structurally normative. Both of these reasons are potentially damaging to Propp's founding assumptions in the *Morphology*. The latter implies that it is harder than Propp assumes to describe a 'universal' formal structure that is absolutely independent of content and context; the former suggests that Propp's selection of data has led him to describe, not all folk narratives, but only one kind of folk narrative.

This criticism is part and parcel of the larger charge laid against Propp: that his data sample (only a hundred narratives) is too small to account for the full range and diversity of folk-narrative structures from diverse contexts. The justice of this charge depends upon our perception of what it is that Propp intended his morphology to do. If Propp's goal is only to describe the morphology of the Russian fairy tale with male protagonists as it is manifested in a single collection from the mid-nineteenth century, then his sample of a hundred narratives from Afanás'ev's collection is sufficient. It is clear, however, from several of Propp's observations that his ambitions are greater than this. In his closing comments concerning his list of functions, for instance, he suggests that his model will hold true, not just for nineteenth-century Russian tales, but 'for the action of a great many other tales of the most dissimilar peoples' (Propp 1968: 64). Propp's selection, however, is not broad enough to warrant a claim that the morphology is capable of describing more than Russian tales of a particular cultural provenance. He does not analyse fairy tales from diverse cultures, and so is unable to discover whether the morphology of tales differ from culture to culture; neither does he analyse tales of diverse periods, thus preventing himself from establishing whether or not morphology changes over time and in accordance with cultural or epistemic historical shifts.

THE STRUCTURALIST CRITIQUE OF PROPP'S *MORPHOLOGY*

One of the earliest theoreticians to develop a sustained critique of Propp's model was the French anthropologist Claude Lévi-Strauss (1908–2009), who responded to the first English translation of Propp's *Morphology* (1958) in a long review published in 1960. Prior to the English translation of Propp's work, as Lévi-Strauss records, his arguments had been unknown in Western Europe and the United States. Lévi-Strauss, therefore, prefaces his critique by commending Propp for the power with which his work anticipates developments in thinking about narrative that had occurred independently outside Russia between 1910 and 1958. 'Those among us who first approached the structural analysis of oral literature around 1950, without direct knowledge of Propp's attempts a quarter of a century earlier,' Lévi-Strauss writes, 'recognize there, to their amazement, formulae – sometimes even whole sentences – that they know well enough they have not borrowed from him' (Lévi-Strauss 1984: 175). This praise for Propp, however, does not prevent Lévi-Strauss from formulating 'certain reservations', the principal of which concerns Propp's efforts to define form 'by opposition to content' (175). Propp, Lévi-Strauss complains, 'divides oral literature in two', separating out 'a form, which is of prime importance because it lends itself to morphological study, and an arbitrary content, which, just because it is arbitrary, he treats as less important' (179). Form and content, however, cannot be separated so easily; they are, Lévi-Strauss insists, 'of the same nature, amenable to the same type of analysis. Content receives its reality from structure, and what is called form is a way of organising the local structures that make up this content' (179). In elaboration of this, Lévi-Strauss invites readers to consider the variable use of the plum tree and the apple tree in Native American narratives. In a Proppian analysis, the use of one or other of these trees – indeed, the use of the tree itself – would be an irrelevance, because such variable features of 'content' would be discounted in favour of an underlying 'formal' function that would remain constant for both plum trees and apple trees. The trouble with this argument, Lévi-Strauss notes, is that each tree does not constitute an 'opaque element' in the Native American cultures that these narratives spring from; they have different kinds of significance, and these different significances give them different kinds of structural role. An 'inventory of contexts,' Lévi-Strauss records, 'reveals that philosophically speaking, what interests natives about the plum tree is its fecundity, while the apple tree attracts the attention because of the strength and depth of its roots' (182). Apple trees will therefore appear in narratives requiring the 'positive function' of fecundity; plum trees in narratives requiring a 'negative function, earth-sky transition' (182). The choice of one tree over another, in other words, will not be random, but will be determined by factors apparent both in the structure of oppositions within a narrative and in the structure of oppositions current within the societies from which these stories derive. Thus Propp's twin contentions, that 'permutability of contents' is 'arbitrary' (182), and that an understanding of content and context is not necessary to an appreciation of form, are exploded.

Lévi-Strauss also develops the argument that, because Propp fails to see that narratives dramatise '**binary oppositions**' which are present in any cultural consciousness, he also fails to present a sufficiently dynamic structural account of the narrative system. In Lévi-Strauss's own reinterpretation of Propp's morphology, accordingly, he rejects the notion that narrative functions exist only in a linear sequence along a chronological axis, and argues instead that narrative functions, drawn from across the chronology of the narrative, can be bundled together, either as oppositions or as transformations of one another (183). Thus, where Propp's analysis reads the functions of 'prohibition' ('don't open that locked door') and 'violation' (the locked door is opened) as purely sequential events, the structuralist analysis treats 'the "violation" as the reverse of the "prohibition" and the latter as a negative transformation of the "injunction"' (183). Likewise, where Propp regards the 'departure' of the hero as an event that merely precedes the hero's return, the structuralist reads 'departure' and 'return' 'as the negative and positive expressions of the same disjunctive function' (183).

If narrative were understood in these more complex terms, Lévi-Strauss contends, it would be possible to replace Propp's 'chronological scheme, in which the order of succession of events is a feature of the structure' with 'another scheme ... which would present a structural model defined as the group of transformations of a small number of elements' (183). This scheme, according to Lévi-Strauss, 'would appear as a matrix with two, three or more dimensions', not unlike a musical score that works both on a chronological (horizontal) axis, and on a structural (vertical) axis, with distinct themes echoing, balancing and modifying one another throughout the composition (183).

Influenced by Lévi-Strauss, subsequent structuralist analysts of the folk and fairy tale have offered modifications of Propp's system along these lines. A. J. Greimas, in *Sémantique Structurale* (1966; *Structural Semantics*), reassembles Propp's 'spheres of action', which he reidentifies as six *actants*, into paired oppositions, and on the basis of these oppositions develops an 'actantial model' that arranges narrative around three axes: the axis of desire in which the 'subject' (the hero) seeks for the 'object' (the sought-for person); the axis of power in which the 'helper' seeks to assist in the subject's attainment of the object whilst the 'opponent' seeks to retard it; and the axis of knowledge in which the 'sender' dispatches the subject on his quest for the object whilst the 'receiver' becomes the beneficiary of this process (Greimas 1983: 200–7; Hébert 2006). Claude Brémond, in 'Morphology of the French Folktale' (1970), also rejects Propp's 'unilinear' series of functions and instead develops a three-dimensional 'dendrogrammattic' flow-chart system designed to show that there are possibilities for choice in the development of a narrative (Rosenberg 1991: 95–97;

Benson 2003: 37). In each case, these models exhibit the crucial feature that distinguishes structuralist analysis from formalist analysis: they reject the system that presents elements of a narrative as static or independent from one another, and replace it with a structural 'matrix' system in which functions are positioned in dynamic relationships.

NARRATIVE SKELETONS

In shifting the focus of folk-narrative analysis from the **diachronic** study of origins and development to the **synchronic** study of narrative mechanics, structuralist and formalist critics changed the kinds of question that were being asked of the fairy tale. The nineteenth-century questions *Where does it come from?* and *How does it travel?* were supplanted by the formal questions: *How does it work? What are its component parts?* and *How do its component parts work together to generate meaning?* Underlying these questions is the hypothesis that fairy tales work like languages, and can be analysed using the same methods that are applied to the study of language by structural linguists: they can be decomposed into their component parts, the parts of the tale can be named, the function of each part can be understood, and, through this process, a clear mechanical picture of the *grammar* of narrative can be built up. The fairy tale is thus stripped back and rebuilt like a machine, or, to remain true to Propp's organic metaphor, dissected like a flower.

For some readers, this scientific dissection of the folk tale invokes the kind of dismay that Lang felt upon first reading Marion Roalfe Cox's groundbreaking study *Cinderella: 345 Variants*, one of the first attempts to classify a fairy-tale type. 'I was horrified at the sight of these skeletons of the tale,' wrote Lang mournfully:

> It was as if one had a glimpse into the place where Hop o' my Thumb's Giant kept the bones of his little victims. Dry bones of child-like and charming tales are these, a place of many skulls.
>
> (Cox 1893: vii)

More recently, Alan Dundes has reiterated this anxiety, urging folklorists to guard against what he calls '**superorganicism**': a tendency towards abstract thinking that 'divides folklore into folk and lore with the emphasis decidedly upon the lore' (Dundes 2007: 130). Formalist and structuralist accounts of fairy tale, however, do not inevitably detract from our understanding of the fairy tale as a form of expression rooted in human social contexts, or from our appreciation of the fairy tale as a creative and imaginative act. Stephen Benson, in his important study of fairy tale and narrative theory, *Cycles of Influence*, has demonstrated that formal and structural theory both develops out of, and feeds back into, creative engagements with the genre (Benson 2003: 41). Alan Dundes, likewise, having voiced his precautions against superorganic thinking, proceeds to describe a three-dimensional structuralism that aims to understand the form of the folk tale, not as 'an end in itself', but as a means of achieving 'a better understanding of the nature of human beings, or at least of a particular society of humans' (Dundes 2007: 136). This more vital form of structuralist analysis becomes possible, Dundes argues, when the formal questions asked of the folk tale (*how does it work?*) are combined with a further set of questions directed at society and the self: *What does it tell us about the human mind? How does it act upon readers mentally? How does it contribute to the fashioning of social and cultural outlooks?* These are the questions posed by psychoanalysis and by socio-cultural analysis, which will be pursued further in the next chapter.

5

PSYCHOANALYSIS, HISTORY AND IDEOLOGY

TWENTIETH- AND TWENTY-FIRST-CENTURY APPROACHES TO FAIRY TALE

Two theoretical approaches to fairy tale have dominated recent critical thinking about the genre: the psychoanalytical and the socio-historical. Neither approach is in any sense unified and neither establishes a singular method of interpretation, but each formulates a powerful proposition concerning the fairy tale that has come to shape creative and critical responses to it in recent decades. Psychoanalysis proposes that fairy tales contain **latent** meanings that derive from the unconscious parts of the human mind, and that the interpretation of fairy tales can bring to light the latent desires and anxieties that such fictions conceal; socio-historical approaches argue that fairy tales are implicated in the political and social belief systems of the societies that have mediated them, and that they express those belief systems in both overt and covert forms. This chapter examines both these propositions, exploring the roots of psychoanalytic thinking about fairy tale in the work of Sigmund Freud and Carl Gustav Jung, the popularisation of the psychoanalytic approach to fairy tales in influential texts such as Bruno Bettelheim's *The Uses of Enchantment* (1976 [Bettelheim 1978]), and the development of socio-historical and Marxist approaches to fairy tale in the work of prominent contemporary theorists such as Jack Zipes.

In part, this critical history is one of disagreement and disputes. Psychoanalysis, especially in the early stages of its conceptual formation, intimated that the fairy tale is a narrative form that is primarily concerned with the unchanging verities of the inner life of man, whilst cultural historians such as Robert Darnton criticised psychoanalysis for its want of historical perspective and for its ignorance of the textual specificities of fairy tales (Darnton 2001: 10–15). These two conceptual approaches, however, have not remained exclusive alternatives, but have increasingly been combined by scholars to create a form of analysis that is complex, stratified and integrated, drawing simultaneously upon the psychologist's understanding of the ways in which fairy tales function at the latent levels to shape identity, and the historian's recognition that the forms of identity that the fairy tale shapes are not timeless and universal, but culturally specific, and ideologically mutable. This psycho-historical form of analysis is widely practised in contemporary fairy-tale studies, and is exemplified in the work of scholars such as Zipes (1997: 39–60), Dundes (1989: 192–236) and Tatar (2006). It is represented at the end of this chapter by the collaborative work of two of the method's pioneers: Sandra Gilbert and Susan Gubar.

PSYCHOANALYSIS AND FAIRY TALE

Psychoanalytical theorists are attracted to fairy tale, and fairy-tale theorists are attracted to psychoanalysis, because the fairy tale is seen as having a privileged connection to the unconscious. This belief lies at the root of both Freudian and Jungian approaches to the fairy tale and so constitutes what may be regarded as the defining assumption of the psychoanalytic method in the field of folk-narrative analysis. In practice, however, Freudian and Jungian interpretations of the fairy tale can differ widely because each method makes quite different assumptions about what the uncon-scious is. For the Freudian, the unconscious is concerned with the formation of the human subject as the locus of repressed forces and the latent meanings of fairy tales must therefore be sought in the repressed unconscious desires of particular human subjects. For the Jungian, the unconscious has a collective dimension, so the meaning of fairy tales must be discovered in the grand universal archetypes that have shaped the thinking of all humanity from the earliest stages of consciousness. Both kinds of analysis will be represented in the following pages, but the first words belong properly to the founder of the school of thought, Sigmund Freud.

The bulk of Freud's direct reflection on fairy tale occurs in four publications that appeared between 1911 and 1918: the pamph-let *Träume im Folklore* (*Dreams in Folklore*; written with David Ernest Oppenheim in 1911, published 1958); the essay 'Märchenstoffe in Träumen' ('The Occurrence in Dreams of Material from Fairy Tales'; 1913); the essay 'Das Motiv der Kästchenwahl' ('The Theme of the Three Caskets'; 1913); and the case study *Aus der geschichte einer infantilen neurose* ('From the History of an Infantile Neurosis'; 1914, published 1918). In these works, Freud is pri-marily concerned to examine how folk narratives and fairy tales corroborate his speculations about the meaning of symbolism in dreams. Fairy tale, for Freud, supplies a common and resonant lexicon of images onto which unconscious wishes and anxieties are displaced, and the analysis of fairy-tale elements in dreams may therefore become a means by which the analyst gains insights into the workings of the patient's unconscious mind. This is nowhere better illustrated than in the case studies he describes in his essay 'The Occurrence in Dreams of Material from Fairy Tales', in which he seeks to explore the appearance of fairy-tale images in the dreams of two of his patients, one of whom is a young, newly married woman who has come to him for treatment of a nervous condition. Freud describes the dream of the young woman as follows:

> *She was in a room that was entirely brown. A little door led to the top of a steep staircase, and up this staircase there came into the room a curious manikin – small, with white hair, a bald top to his head and a red nose. He danced round the room in front of her, carried on in the funniest way,*

and then went down the staircase again. He was dressed in a grey garment, through which every part of his figure was visible.

(Freud 1958a: 281, italics in original)

In the course of analysis, the woman reveals that the manikin, as well as resembling her father-in-law, brings to mind the story of 'Rumpelstiltskin', 'who danced around in the same funny way'. She also reveals that she associates the brown room with the idea of beds (281–82). Freud's analysis tackles the dream on several fronts. Knowing that the young woman is experiencing anxieties concerning her recent marriage, he proposes that the brown room is the marital bedroom, and that the presence of the manikin in the dream is a disguised recollection of her husband's visit to their double bed 'to play his part' (282). He also suggests that, at a deeper level, the dream is a codified meditation on the sexual act itself: the brown room is symbolic of the vagina, the 'little man' is a penis, and the woman's description of a 'narrow door and … steep stairs' confirm the view 'that the situation was a representation of intercourse' (282). The specific anxieties that have brought this imagery into play, Freud speculates, are the issues concerning conception that have preoccupied his patient, an interpretation that is given additional reinforcement by the fact that the woman describes the 'little man' as wearing a 'transparent grey garment' like a condom (282). '[A]mong the instigating causes of the dream,' Freud therefore judges, are 'considerations of preventing conception and worries whether the visit of her husband's might not have sown the seed of a second child' (282–83). The fairy tale of 'Rumpelstiltskin', in this context, is, according to Freud, connected with these 'contemporary thoughts underlying the dream … by a neat antithetic relation':

In the fairy tale [Rumpelstiltskin] comes in order to take away the queen's first child. In the dream the little man comes in the shape of a father, because he had presumably brought a second child.

(Freud 1958a: 283)

The figure of Rumpelstiltskin thus reinforces (by inversion) her wishes about conception: the fairy tale is about the attempted seizure of a child by a small man; the dream uses this idea to express, in coded form, anxieties about the delivery of a child. Understood in these terms, Freud observes, it is also possible to read the figure of Rumpelstiltskin in the dream as a **symbol** connected to 'the deeper, infantile stratum of the dream-thoughts'. 'The droll little fellow, whose very name is unknown, whose secret is so eagerly canvassed, who can perform such extraordinary tricks' (283) leads Freud inexorably to the same conclusion that his disciple Géza Róheim makes in his assessment of the Rumpelstiltskin story 36 years later. 'May we make a daring guess and like the princess in the story reveal the name of the dwarf?' asks Róheim. We may, he concludes immediately: 'It is Penis' (Róheim 1992: 127).

Freud's interest in these manifestations of imagery from fairy tales is motivated exclusively by what it might tell him about his patient's preoccupations. He is a clinician first and foremost, and interpretations of fairy tales are therefore motivated by their clinical relevance: the dream, he believes, represents a release, in censored form, of the unconscious wishes of his patient, and it seizes upon common, resonant imagery such as that found in fairy tale as a means of both expressing and concealing hidden wishes. The interpretation of the fairy tale, in this respect, is of significance for Freud only insofar as it can give him information about the mental state of his patient.

On some occasions, however, Freud also make the tantalising, but invariably brief, suggestion that an investigation of the ways in which fairy-tale symbolism appears in dreams might also form the basis of an understanding of fairy tales as independently existing narratives. For instance, after concluding that the Rumpelstiltskin-like figure in the dream of his young married patient symbolises her sexual anxieties, Freud notes that '[i]f we carefully observe from clear instances the way in which dreamers use fairy tales and the point at which they bring them in, we may perhaps also succeed in picking up some hints which will help in interpreting remaining obscurities *in the fairy tales themselves*' (Freud 1958a: 283, italics added). Similarly, after drawing a parallel between a young man's fear of wolves and his fear of his father in the case study of 'The Wolf Man', Freud raises the question of whether 'infantile fear of the father' may not also be 'the hidden content' of fairy tales such as 'The Wolf and the Seven Kids' and 'Little Red Riding Hood' (Freud 1958a: 286–87). It is, in other words, conceivable for Freud, so long as sufficient interpretative caution is exercised, to make the conceptual leap from claiming that a fairy-tale image has a particular and oft-repeated meaning in the dreams of particular human subjects, to claiming that the image has the same symbolic meaning in the fairy tale. Several of Freud's followers, notably Ernest Jones, Géza Róheim and Bruno Bettelheim, have made precisely this conceptual leap, in the process making a transition from the patient-focused analysis of Freud's case studies, to types of analysis that find symbolism in a text independent of the psychology of a particular producer. Freud remains more tentative, as we may see from the hesitancy of his formulation of this idea above and from the fact that he is careful to suggest that any symbolic reading of fairy tales should regard the symbolism that appears in them as having context-specific meanings rather than universal meanings ('if we carefully observe from clear instances the way in which dreamers use fairy tales … '). Nevertheless, Freud does on occasion allow himself to assume – 'boldly assume', he writes – that the forms of 'symbolic substitution' that he finds in dreams can also occur in fairy tales, thus allowing interpreters of fairy tale to postulate (or 'boldly assume') that fairy tales can be read symbolically using the same methods that Freud uses for dreams.

This assumption is made most courageously by Freud in his speculative essay 'The Theme of the Three Caskets', in which he reflects upon the general significances of the motif of the third daughter that appears in modified forms in *King Lear*, 'Cinderella', the tale of Cupid and Psyche, and the story of the choice between three caskets in *The Merchant of Venice* (in the last case, Freud argues that the three caskets in Shakespeare's play are symbolic of '*a man's choice between three women*'; Freud 1958b: 292). Surveying various applications of this motif, Freud poses the question: 'who are these three sisters and why must the choice fall on the third?' (293), by which he means to ask, not who they are at the manifest level of the plot, but who they are in terms of their latent significance. In framing an answer he provides what may be regarded as an indicative psychoanalytic reading of a popular traditional tale.

His analysis runs as follows: the youngest woman in these fictions is often silent, or she is concealed, or she makes herself plain. This suggests to Freud that one of the primary characteristics of the 'third one' is her quietness or, indeed, her dumbness, a concept that 'in dreams ... is a common representation of death' (295). Other elements of these tales suggest the same theme to Freud:

> Hiding and being unfindable – a thing which confronts the prince in the fairy tale of Cinderella three times, is another symbol of death in dreams; so, too, is a marked pallor, of which the 'paleness' of the lead in one reading of Shakespeare's [*The Merchant of Venice*] is a reminder.
>
> (Freud 1958b: 295)

'These indications,' Freud concludes, suggest that 'the third one of the sisters between whom the choice is made is a dead woman' – and may even stand for 'Death itself, the Goddess of Death'. If the third is the Goddess of Death, moreover, then all the sisters 'are known to us': '[t]hey are the Fates, the Moerae, the Parcae or the Norns, the third of whom is called Atropos the inexorable' (296). This conclusion, Freud concedes, may appear to introduce a contradiction into the story: why would the figure of death appear as a beloved object, and why would the protagonist willingly choose death? The contradiction, however, is resolved according to Freud if we recall that 'Man ... makes use of his imaginative activity in order to satisfy the wishes that reality does not satisfy' (299). Appalled by the 'truth embodied in the myth of the Moerae' that death is the destiny of all men, an alternative story has been constructed – the story of Cinderella, of Lear or the Three Caskets – 'in which the Goddess of Death was replaced by the Goddess of Love and by what was equivalent to her in human shape' (299). The tale thus becomes a complicated form of denial and consolation: a 'wishful reversal' in which ideas that threaten the ego are alchemically metamorphosed into their opposite: 'the fairest, best, most desirable and most loveable of women' (299).

In this way, Freud answers his own question and establishes a broader principle for psychoanalytic interpretation: the true meaning of myths and fairy tales does not reside in their manifest content, which is often enough nonsensical, but in their latent significances for the unconscious mind, at which level of meaning the apparent 'difficulties' or 'absurdities' of popular narrative traditions resolve themselves into another story that has a coherent and rationally explicable meaning. One story underlies another like strata in rock formations, and the diligent analyst-archaeologist, using free association as a tool, may scrape away the surface layers to reveal the deeper, and Freud suggests *more true*, foundations beneath.

A pressing question raised by Freud's analysis of 'Cinderella' concerns the mentality that is under investigation in these interrogations of the underlying strata of meaning. *Who is the patient on the couch?* This question is easy enough to answer in Freud's case studies, since these take, as their subject matter, the fantasies of a specific patient. But in literary or textual criticism it becomes much harder to identify whose unconscious desires are being analysed. Is the 'unconscious' under analysis that of the particular originator of a tale, or the entirety of the 'folk' that produced that tale, or any one person or group of people for whom that tale becomes meaningful, or, more simply, all of humanity? The kinds of responses given to this question will depend partly upon whether the analyst of fairy tale is Freudian or Jungian by inclination. The Freudian, whether implicitly (Freud himself) or explicitly (Géza Róheim), concedes that the fairy tale and the myth reflect a form of collective identity, but maintains that such narratives have only become repositories for collective experience because they deal with drives, desires and developmental patterns that are commonly experienced by many or all individually (Róheim 1992: 6). Jungians, by contrast, argue that certain symbols in dreams and in fairy tales are universal because they are archetypal and derive from an unconscious that is primarily collective. It is this archetypal and collective character of the symbolism in fairy tales that, for the Jungian, explains their recurrent patterns and their widespread presence in societies throughout the world. It is, furthermore, the archetypal and collective character of the imagery of myths and fairy tales that justifies our attribution to them of universal meanings that transcend individual psychological concerns and embrace psychic experiences that are fundamental to all humanity. This difference between Freudian and Jungian attitudes to the unconscious leads to a broad distinction in both schools' understanding of what it is that the fairy tale expresses on the latent level. Freudians tend to see fairy tales as illustrative of the personal struggle for identity, especially as it is manifested in the drive for sexual definition and its corresponding anxieties. Thus Ernest Jones sees the story of 'The Frog King' as a narrative expressing a 'maiden's gradual overcoming of her aversion to intimacy' with the 'male organ' (Jones 1951: 16). And elsewhere, Geza Róheim reads the plucking of hairs from the devil's head in 'Three Golden Hairs of the Devil' as expressive of the covert Oedipal desire of the son to castrate the father (Róheim 1992: 8–9). Jungian readings, by contrast, tend to present fairy tales as being part of a grander narrative about mankind, not so much concerned with the local struggles on the path to individual identity, as with the great spiritual quest of the human soul for which these individual or local struggles stand as paradigms. Thus, Joseph Campbell reads 'The Frog King' not only as a narrative concerned with 'the coming of adolescence' (though it is that), but also as a manifestation of the 'call to adventure' that initiates the archetypal – and therefore universal – quest of the hero (Campbell 1993: 51). Marie von Franz, in another example of a Jungian approach to fairy tale, reads the story of the 'The Three Feathers' in Grimm as a narrative that expresses the psychic necessity for a patriarchal society 'ruled by rigid principles' to attain spiritual renewal by reconnecting with a 'feminine element' that has been suppressed (von Franz 1996: 64). For one school of thought, the sexual anxieties of the individual provide the key to the latent meaning of the fairy tale; for the other, the fairy tale is a manifestation of collective unconscious archetypes and, as such, can aid the psyche in its quest for a higher state of selfhood and 'inner renewal' (Bettelheim 1978: 36).

FAIRY MEDICINE: BRUNO BETTELHEIM AND READER-FOCUSED ANALYSIS

Two possible directions for the psychoanalytical study of fairy tale have been considered above: the patient-orientated analysis in which the narrative becomes an item of evidence in the investigation of the unconscious mental life of a specific person; and the text-orientated analysis, in which the narrative of the fairy tale becomes evidence that patterns of mental development or psychic structures are deeply embedded in products of human imagination and culture more generally. If it may legitimately be claimed that the former clinical practice offers a mandate for literary-critical practices, the closest equivalent to these patient-orientated analyses must be those critical studies that use the work of a writer or storyteller or collector as an item of evidence in the investigation of his or her unconscious mental life. These approaches are relatively rare in fairy-tale studies because fairy tales are generally regarded as authorless texts, or, at least, texts whose significance transcends the psychology of any one mediator. Such approaches do exist, however, especially in studies of works or collections associated with a specific name or group of names. Into this category might fall Zipes's argument that the collecting practices of the Grimms, and their refashioning of the tales 'according to their needs and ethical notions of the pure German language' were 'essentially an act of compensation' for the early death of their father, and for the threat posed to Germany by Napoleonic imperialism (in McGlathery 1988: 214). We might also include in this category Jackie Wullschlager's analysis of Hans Christian Andersen's 'The Little Mermaid', in which the mermaid figure, trapped half way between land and sea, the upper-world and the lower-world, body and spirit, is interpreted as Andersen's neurotic attempt to negotiate feelings of bisexuality (Wullschlager 2001: 167–68). Author-focused analytical readings, however, are less common in the study of folk narrative and fairy tale than they are in the study of other forms of fiction. More commonly, analyses of fairy tales are either akin to the analysis that Freud makes of 'Cinderella' in which the text is psychoanalysed, or else they fall into a third category: the reader- or hearer-focused analysis, in which the fairy tale becomes a fiction that has functional value, as a means of communicating with recipients of the text at a profound unconscious level about processes of personal and social development. By far the best-known practitioner of this kind of analysis, and perhaps the best-known psychoanalytical theorist of the fairy tale altogether, is Bruno Bettelheim, whose 1976 work *The Uses of Enchantment: The Meaning and Importance of Fairy Tales* has served both to popularise psychoanalytical approaches to fairy tale and to transform attitudes to the value of fairy tales as a form of children's literature.

Bettelheim's central thesis in *The Uses of Enchantment* is that fairy tales are good for children because they assist the child in negotiating unconscious anxieties and developmental difficulties in an unthreatening and non-confrontational manner. Fairy tales, Bettelheim argues, address the child's unconscious needs in a symbolic language that 'conforms to the way a child thinks and experiences the world' (Bettelheim 1978: 45); they are, therefore, narratives that can serve as therapeutic tools, that can help guide the child along the perilous unconscious terrain of growing up. In Bettelheim's words:

> Fairy tales, unlike any other form of literature, direct the child to discover his identity and calling, and they also suggest what experiences are needed to develop his character further. Fairy tales intimate that a rewarding, good life is within one's reach despite adversity – but only if one does not shy away from the hazardous struggles without which one can never achieve true identity. These stories promise that if a child dares to engage in this fearsome and taxing search, benevolent powers will come to his aid, and he will succeed.
>
> (Bettelheim 1978: 24)

Bettelheim's reading of 'Jack and the Beanstalk' may serve as an illustration of his approach. This story, Bettelheim argues, engages with the Oedipal struggle of the 'pubertal boy' to detach himself from infantile dependence on an unsympathetic mother and to define himself instead as a mature individual who can take possession of the powers of the father (Bettelheim 1978: 184). Jack begins the story, Bettelheim observes, in an infantile state, dependent upon the mother and upon the milk that is given by the cow, Milky White, symbolic, Bettelheim notes, of the mother's breast (187). He is, however, expelled from this 'infantile paradise' by the mother (the milk runs out), which causes him to turn to a father figure, 'represented in the story by the man encountered on the way' (187–88). This father figure supplies him with the magic beans that grow the beanstalk; in symbolic terms, the seed capable of giving him phallic potency. But when Jack returns home, his mother, not yet believing in his masculine potency, derides 'Jack's belief in the magic power of his seeds' which leads him to indulge in the 'fantasy satisfaction' of a 'belief in magic phallic powers as symbolised by the huge beanstalk' (187 and 189). This progression from the 'oral phase' to the 'phallic phase' 'permits Jack to engage in oedipal conflict with the ogre': he climbs the beanstalk, confronts the giant, steals what he needs to become self-sufficient, and engages in a final struggle with his enemy 'which he survives and finally wins, thanks only to the oedipal mother's taking his side against her own husband'. Having won this battle, Jack is, at the conclusion of the tale, able to relinquish 'his reliance on the belief in the magic power of phallic self-assertion', symbolised by the cutting down of the beanstalk, and this act in turn 'opens the way towards a development of mature masculinity' (187).

Interpretative readings of the kind performed by Bettelheim are seductive. They are ingenious in their capacity to map the evidence of the story onto the developmental patterns described by analysts, and they invariably capture something of the 'family romance' that fairy tales typically reflect: the rivalry of sibling and sibling, the contest for authority between son and father, the envy of the stepmother for her new partner's existing children, the suspicion of the mother-in-law for her son's affianced bride, the competition of daughter and mother for attention of the patriarchal father, the illicit desire of father for daughter, and the yearning of the developing young girl or boy to be somewhere else, with other people, in other clothes and other climes, looking forward to a glittering future of wealth and happiness. All of this is undeniably the primary narrative material of the fairy tale. The seductions of Bettelheim's readings, however, should not blind us to their limitations. In the first place, as Robert Darnton (1984 [Darnton 2001]) and Maria Tatar (1992) have argued, many of the elements in these stories that Bettelheim regards as submerged and therefore 'unconscious' were likely to have been explicit in the peasant tales from which they derive. In translating oral tales into printed texts for children, Tatar maintains, nineteenth-century collectors of fairy tales collaborated, 'wittingly and unwittingly', 'in a cultural project of silencing sexuality and suppressing all allusions to bodily functions' (Tatar 1992: 65). They re-wrote the tales to eliminate 'bawdy episodes or scatological humour,' or they collected the tales from informants who, confronted with 'scholarly' and 'solemn' folklorists, supplied 'cleaned-up versions from the very start' (65). Fairy tales, according to this analysis, do not have covert sexual contents because they reflect the contents of the unconscious mind; they have covert sexual contents because sexual elements that were once explicit and intentional have been masked by a sustained cultural process of indirect censorship and bowdlerisation.

A second recurrent concern voiced by scholars about Bettelheim's fairy-tale analysis is that he does not have a developed understanding of the history or the cultural provenance of the narratives he uses. In the reading above, he treats 'Jack and the Beanstalk' as though it is a stable narrative, with stable significances; but a folklorist would be aware that there are many variants of this tale, each of which are different from one another, and each of which invite different kinds of reading. For instance, in Joseph Jacobs's 1890 version of the story, Jack steals from the giant, first a bag of money, then the hen that lays golden eggs and finally the magic harp. Bettelheim, who appears to be using Jacobs as a source, argues that this sequence is logical because of its symbolic significance: the immature ego first acquires the resources that it needs for its immediate satisfaction; it then learns that 'one runs out of things if one cannot produce them' so it obtains a means of ensuring that 'all physical needs are … permanently satisfied'; finally, having ensured physical satisfaction, it reaches for 'something better than mere material goods': 'the golden harp, which symbolizes beauty, art, the higher things in life' (Bettelheim 1978: 191). Bettelheim, however, is unaware of the version of the story recorded by E. S. Hartland in the same year as Jacobs's version, in which Jack steals the objects in a different order (Hartland 2000: 35–44). Presumably, if Bettelheim had stumbled, by chance, upon Hartland's version, instead of stumbling, by chance, upon Jacobs's version, his reading would have had to be different. But what does this variation say about psychoanalytic interpretations? Should we argue that the psychoanalytic interpretation must be different for each variant of the tale, and that tales *do not* therefore represent timeless or archetypal verities, but textually and contextually variable ones? Or should we argue, as Bettelheim attempts to do, that, in such cases, one version of the story must be more 'authentic' than the other, the authentic one being that which is closest to the folk source? If the latter, we will certainly face methodological difficulties with this story, since both Jacobs's version and Hartland's versions are literary works, and are at least partly derived from the chapbook tradition of eighteenth- and nineteenth-century Britain. In such cases, the 'folk' original that Bettelheim seeks to analyse seems very remote.

This critique of Bettelheim is made forcefully by Darnton; psychoanalysts, he notes, regard symbolism as the key with which stories can be unlocked, but many of the elements that psycho-analysts have made so much of in their interpretations of fairy tales do not appear in the peasant versions of these stories. Erich Fromm's analysis of 'Little Red Riding Hood' (Fromm 1957: 240–41) depends upon the interpretation of key symbols such as the 'red hood' that features in Perrault's literary fiction; as folk-lorists now know, however, such symbols are not found in French peasant versions of the story (Darnton 2001: 10–11). Likewise, Bettelheim emphasises the latent importance of the huntsman's arrival with his phallic weapon to deliver a 'happy ending' in 'Little Red Riding Hood'; but he ignores, or is ignorant of, the fact that this particular 'happy ending', prior to the literary manipulation of the story by the Grimms and their informants, was not a constitutive feature of the tale (Darnton 2001: 12–13). In such approaches to the fairy tale, Darnton laments, Bettelheim reveals himself to be blind 'to the historical dimension of folk-tales': 'He treats them, so to speak, flattened out, like patients on a couch, in a timeless contemporaneity' and 'does not question their origins or worry over other meanings that they might have had in other contexts because he knows how the soul works and how it has always worked' (Darnton 2001: 11 and 13).

Bettelheim's disregard of the history and the cultural specificity of the versions of the narratives he deals with gives rise to a fur-ther objection to his work: that in failing to recognise that these narratives are products of specific histories, he fails to recognise that the models of identity formation that they encode are also culturally and historically specific. Bettelheim reads 'Jack and the Beanstalk' as a story in which a developing young man is encouraged to define himself antagonistically to his mother, and to attain masculine identity by entering a conflictual relationship with his father. This pattern of development, for Bettelheim, is normal and healthy, and one that fairy tales ought to instil in young auditors. Read through the lens of social and cultural history, however, the model of identity prescribed in Jacobs's 'Jack and the Beanstalk', far from being normative, may be seen as a reflection of very specific social codes; namely, the patriarchal and imperialistic codes that were dominant in eighteenth- and nineteenth-century Britain when the versions of the narrative that Bettelheim uses were inscribed (Szumsky 1999: 21–22; Teverson 2010: 213–14). Through the figure of Jack, the young reader is encouraged to see the resources of the world in terms of appropriation, conquest and control; he is persuaded to regard women as figures who supply him with his wants but against whom he must ultimately define himself; and he is offered a mode of male behaviour that is based upon aggression and conflict. To insist, in the late twentieth century, that such models of behaviour should be used uncritically to shape the characters of the young, or, worse, to claim that they are 'archetypal' and therefore immutable, is not, as many of Bettelheim's critics have observed, to liberate youthful auditors of the tale, but to constrain them by forcing them into the strait-jacket identities that suit the interests of authoritarian power structures. This argument lies at the root of the critique of Bettelheim framed by Jack Zipes in his 1977 essay 'On the Use and Abuse of Folk and Fairy Tales with Children: Bruno Bettelheim's Moralistic Magic Wand' (reworked and extended in the light of new evidence in 2002). Bettelheim, Zipes argues, 'fails to take into account that the symbols and patterns of the tales reflect specific forms of social behaviour and activity' and so makes the scholarly, and indeed ethical, error of presenting fairy tales as models of universal norms (Zipes 2002: 190; see also Haase 1999).

HISTORIES FROM BELOW: HISTORICISM AND THE FAIRY TALE

The contestation of the early psychoanalytic approach to fairy tale has, in the main, been conducted by folklorists, historians and cultural materialists who have sought to reaffirm the importance of understanding fairy tales in their historical context. The fairy tale, these scholars and theorists argue, is not a psychodrama of the human soul mediating timeless truths about our inner selves. It is a form of fiction that, like all forms of fiction, has been shaped by the cultural and historical environments in which it has been disseminated, and mediates the beliefs and the world-views that are current in those environments. Four basic principles underlie this reaffirmation of the historicity of fairy tales. They are, firstly, that fairy tales are historical documents with a specific material past; secondly, that the meanings of fairy tales can only be understood in relation to the cultural contexts in which they have been produced and received; thirdly, that fairy tales do not have stable or universal meanings but mean different things in different contexts; and fourthly, that fairy tales, like all products of human culture, are not 'innocent' or 'naive', but reflect the priorities – the 'world-views', 'ideologies' or mentalités – of the cultures that have shaped them. Together these principles comprise what may be called a 'historicist' approach to fairy tales: an approach that comprehends the material dimensions of the folk narrative text and the sociological dimensions of folk-narrative discourse.

This socio-historical approach to fairy tales has been current, in its modern form, since at least 1956, when Lutz Röhrich argued, in *Märchen und Wirklichkeit* (*Folktales and Reality*), that folk narratives may be regarded as 'mirrors of the real world' that reflect the social milieux in which they circulate. 'As marvellous as some elements of the folktale may be,' Röhrich proposed, their 'depiction of social life is never far from the truth': folk-tale narrators continue to use 'their own environment as a model' for fantastical environments such as 'heaven and hell' (Röhrich 1991: 192). A similar argument is offered by the cultural historian Robert Darnton in his essay on French folk tales, 'Peasants Tell Tales: The Meaning of Mother Goose'. Central to Darnton's thesis, and developing from his forthright critique of psychoanalytical approaches, is the proposal that '[t]he great collections of folktales made in the late nineteenth and early twentieth centuries', despite their distance from peasant sources, 'provide a rare opportunity to make contact with the illiterate masses who have disappeared into the past without leaving a trace' (Darnton 2001: 17–18). Focusing upon folk tales referenced in the collection *Le conte populaire Français* by Paul Delarue and Marie-Louise Ténèze (1976–85), Darnton maintains that, through a process of careful comparative analysis of a large body of texts, it is possible to obtain a sense of 'the general outline of a tale as it existed in the oral tradition', and in so doing to recover lost peasant voices from the seventeenth and eighteenth centuries (18). What these lost voices tell us, he argues, confirms historians' judgements about what the world of the European peasant was like during the Enlightenment: it was a world of 'step-mothers and orphans, of inexorable, unending toil, and of brutal emotions, both raw and repressed'; 'lives really were nasty, brutish and short', and surviving folk narratives confirm this reality at every turn (29). In Perrault's 'La petit poucet' ('Little Thumbling') a woodsman and his wife resolve to 'get rid of their children' because they are unable to support them during a famine. By abandoning their children in this way they were 'trying to cope with a problem that overwhelmed the peasantry many times in the seventeenth and eighteenth centuries – the problem of survival during a period of demographic disaster' (30). In 'Chatte botté' ('Puss in Boots') a third son is left with only a cat for his patrimony after his elder brothers have secured the mill and the ass. This scenario, Darnton suggests, would have been familiar given that 'inheritance customs of French peasants, as well as noblemen, often prevented the fragmentation of the patrimony by favouring the eldest son' (29). And so the argument goes on: 'Cinderella' depicts rivalry between stepsiblings because such rivalry for resources would have been inevitable in the economic conditions in which these narratives took shape; depictions of extravagant feasting appear repeatedly because 'to eat or not to eat ... was the question peasants confronted in their folklore as well as in their daily lives' (31–32); and characters go off to seek their fortune because it was a common experience for peasants in 'a real world' to take to the road 'to escape poverty at home and ... find employment in greener pastures' (36). Thus, Darnton concludes:

> whenever one looks behind Perrault to the peasant versions of Mother Goose, one finds elements of realism – not photographic

accounts of life in the barnyard (peasants did not actually have as many children as there are holes in a sieve, and they did not eat them) but a picture that corresponds to everything that social historians have been able to piece together from the archives. The picture fits, and the fit was a matter of consequence. By showing how life was lived, *terre à terre*, in the village and on the road, the tales helped orient the peasants. They mapped the ways of the world and demonstrated the folly of expecting anything more than cruelty from a cruel social order.

(Darnton 2001: 38; see also Tatar 1992: 46–49 and 192–93)

The principal implication of this **Euhemerist** argument is that folk narratives become a means of recovering the world-views, the life experiences, of a disenfranchised class of society whose histories have not been recorded by more conventional means. Elsewhere, this argument has been extended to specific social groups: for example, Marina Warner and Angela Carter have suggested that folk narratives are a means of recovering the voices of the women who have played such an important role in disseminating them (see Carter 1991; Warner 1995: 17–24). It has also been proposed that folk tales are a means of reconstructing the historical outlook of ethnic groups, or national minorities, that have not been represented extensively or favourably in official records. Kamau Brathwaite, for instance, in his pamphlets *Folk Culture of the Slaves in Jamaica* (Brathwaite 1970) and *Wars of Respect: Nanny and Sam Sharpe* (Brathwaite 1977), argues that the narratives of African slaves that have been passed on in oral tradition are one of the few means available to the modern historian of accessing eighteenth- and nineteenth-century slave culture. Writers such as Toni Morrison (1987 [Morrison 1997]) and Patrick Chamoiseau (1988; Chamoiseau 1998), likewise, draw upon oral traditions in their work in an endeavour to recover and rescript the historical experience of slavery from the slave's point of view. Each writer, in different ways, operates on the principle expressed by Brathwaite that:

a nation whose sense of history is basically derived from the history of the struggle of its people, most of whom have been non-literate and have had no formal historians of their own ... must boldly enter

into its unwritten/invisible record, the oral traditions, collective memory
of the people, in order to truly reveal what in fact has been achieved.

(Brathwaite 1977: 5)

VOICE OF THE PEOPLE? MARXISM AND FOLK NARRATIVE

The historicist approach to fairy tales in the twentieth and
twenty-first centuries cannot be understood independently of
Marxist cultural theory. Marxist thinking about the materiality of
culture underwrites the historicist argument that folk narratives
are products of their social and political contexts; it also gives rise
to the view that folk narratives and fairy tales are ideological
battle grounds upon which the hegemonic discourses of those
with cultural authority may either be inscribed or contested. In
recent decades, Marxist attitudes to folk narratives have been,
broadly speaking, affirmative, to the extent that Marxist critics have
tended to see folk and fairy tales as fictions that have 'relatively
autonomous origins within communities' and so represent a form of
'expressive, *shared* ... behaviour' that 'has a far more democratic
distribution than "high" art' (Limón 1983: 39). Marxist valorisation
of folk narratives, however, has developed relatively late in the history of Marxist thought. Until the 1930s at least, the prevailing
current of Marxist theory did not regard folk narratives as pro-
gressive or politically valuable fictions, but, quite the contrary, as
atavistic survivals of obsolete social structures that function to
keep the subaltern classes in a state of ignorance. In Soviet Russia,
in the wake of the Revolution of 1917, the Proletarian Cultural
and Educational Organisations (Proletcul't) 'declared that folklore
was hostile to Soviet people, because it reflected the *kulak* ("rich
farmers") ideology', and the Children's Proletcul't sought to era-
dicate folk tales from primary education 'on the basis that they
glorified tsars and tsareviches, corrupted and instigated sickly fantasies in children, developed the kulak attitude, and strengthened
bourgeois ideals' (Oinas 1978: 77). The Russian Association of
Proletarian Writers (RAPP), as 'heir of the Proletcul't', continued this
same policy towards folklore, arguing that folklore was backward
and should be uprooted (Oinas 1978: 77). This Communist

suspicion of folklore, Limón proposes, left its imprint on Western European forms of Marxism, which have persisted in arguing that folklore is a mode of cultural expression that is in a state of decline, and that is no longer capable of expressing an 'emancipatory and critical politics' because it is 'under constant and competitive attack from the hegemonic sociocultural social order' (Limón 1983: 38–39). This attitude is apparent, Limón observes, in the work of Theodor Adorno, who maintains that 'folklore is a thing of the preindustrial past and today serves only the needs of "objectivist" high art'; it is also present in the work of Walter Benjamin who, in his essay 'The Storyteller' (1936), advances the thesis that 'the art of storytelling is coming to an end' (Limón 1983: 39; Benjamin 1999: 86). Although these Frankfurt School Marxists 'sense the potentially oppositional nature of folklore', they persistently define folklore 'as a largely historical phenomenon associated with precapitalist modes of production, socially marginal sectors, or childhood, and therefore in a process of decline', and where they do 'analyze folklore's contemporary presence as an oppositional force, the character of that opposition is left vague and unspecified' (Limón 1983: 39). Even Antonio Gramsci, who sees folklore in general as a 'conception of the world and life ... in opposition ... to "official" conceptions of the world', argues that folklore should only be taught with a view to uprooting 'what other conceptions of the world and of life' are 'active in the intellectual and moral formation of young people' and replacing them 'with conceptions that are deemed to be superior' (Gramsci 1985: 191; Limón 1983: 42).

Suspicion of folklore within Marxist thought has not remained uncontested however. In Russia, the leading folklorists Azadovskij and J. Sokolov challenged early Soviet hostility to folklore and folk narrative by arguing, contrary to the prevailing opinion, that folk culture was 'not only concerned with the past but also reflected contemporary life' (Oinas 1978: 78). The leading Soviet writer Maxim Gorky also launched a 'powerful appeal' on behalf of folklore at the First Congress of Soviet Writers in 1934, arguing that folklore belonged 'first of all, to working people' and was capable of conveying a 'life optimism' which expressed 'the deepest moral and human aspirations of the masses' (Oinas 1978: 78). This endorsement of folklore by such a major figure as Gorky '[a]s if by magic ... opened the eyes of the party leaders to the possibilities that folklore would have for the advancement of communism', and 'from that time on ... conscious use [was made] of folklore for social and political purposes' in the Soviet Union and the Eastern Bloc (78).

Outside the Soviet context, more affirmative accounts of the political value of folk and fairy tales have also been offered by some Western Marxist thinkers. Ernst Bloch advances the thesis promoted and popularised by Jack Zipes that the fairy tale, even after it has been appropriated and distorted by a rapacious bourgeois culture industry, retains a utopian spirit that makes it capable of expressing revolutionary hope for social and political change (Zipes 2002: 156). Walter Benjamin too, despite his lament for the decline of story-telling in the modern world, proposes that the popular story operates an expressive form of cunning wisdom that may serve as an antidote to the 'information' favoured by an instrumentalised and alienating capitalist economy (Benjamin 1999: 88–89). In making this argument, Benjamin, in anticipation of Roland Barthes, draws a distinction between the 'myth' and the 'fairy tale' as media of socio-political engagement. The myth, he proposes, represents orthodox and authoritarian forms of thinking, the world-view of the powerful; the fairy tale, by contrast, first told in 'the house-hold of humanity', is an expression of the 'counsel' of the common man (100–1):

> The fairy tale tells us of the earliest arrangements that mankind made to shake off the nightmare which the myth had placed upon its chest. In the figure of the fool it shows how mankind 'acts dumb' towards the myth; ... in the figure of the man who sets out to learn what fear is it shows us that the things we are afraid of can be seen through; in the figure of the wiseacre it shows us that the questions posed by the myth are simple minded ... The wisest thing – so the fairy tale taught mankind in olden times, and teaches children to this day – is to meet the forces of the mythical world with cunning and with high spirits ... The liberating magic which the fairy tale has at its disposal does not bring nature into play in a mythical way, but points to its complicity with liberated man.

> (Benjamin 1999: 101)

For both Bloch and Benjamin, therefore, though the 'fairy-tale world ... no longer belongs to the present', 'the mirror of the fairy tale has not become opaque, and the manner of wish-fulfilment which peers forth from it is not entirely without a home' (Bloch, in Zipes 2002: 150–51). 'It all adds up to this,' notes Bloch: 'the fairy tale narrates a wish-fulfilment which is not bound by its own time and the apparel of its contents'. This 'wish-fulfilment,' for Zipes, constitutes 'a special category of *Vor-Schein*': an 'anticipatory illusion' of a better world that can be used to offset the 'instrumental rationalisation' of modern capitalist society and 'to project visions of better worlds which human beings are capable of realising with their own powers' (Zipes 2002: 157–58 and 149).

These Marxist arguments in favour of the utopian and subversive capabilities of folk and fairy tale have faced criticism from a number of perspectives. They are, for instance, at odds with the conception of folk tale subscribed to by many anthropological folklorists, who do not see the folk tale as fulfilling a counter-cultural role in folk contexts, but a deeply conservative one. As William Bascom observed in 1954, one of the four basic functions of folklore is to maintain 'conformity to the accepted patterns of behaviour' by validating and enforcing cultural norms (Bascom 1981: 59). '[F]olklore is employed,' Bascom writes, 'to control, influence, or direct the activities of others from the time the first lullaby is sung or ogre tale is told to them', and it therefore functions as a mechanism for policing established social patterns, not disrupting them (60). Of course, this does not rule out the possibility that folk narratives may involve the performance of dissent. This is implicit in the subject matter of many well-known folk and fairy tales, which, in certain contexts, have operated as fantasies of vengeance and empowerment on the part of the poor. The carnivalesque performance of dissent in folk tales, however, does not necessarily entail a radical political agenda; and may, indeed, function as a consolation and compensation for lack of real power. As Darnton observes, depictions of table-turning in the French tradition do not necessarily amount to Jacobinism:

> No doubt the peasants derived some satisfaction from outwitting the
> rich and powerful in their fantasies as they tried to outwit them in

everyday life, by lawsuits, cheating on manorial dues, and poaching. ...
But it would be vain to search in such fantasies for the germ of
republicanism. To dream of confounding the king by marrying a
princess was hardly to challenge the moral basis of the Old Regime ...
The clever weakling makes a fool of the strong oppressor by raising a
chorus of laughter at his expense. ... But laughter, even Rabelaisian
laughter, has limits. Once it subsides, the tables turn back again; and
as in the succession of lent to Carnival in the unfolding of the calendar
year, the old order regains its hold on the revellers.

(Darnton 2001: 59)

Patrick Chamoiseau, in the introduction to his collection *Au temps
de l'antan: Contes du pays Martinique* (1988; published in the UK
as *Strange Words* and in the USA as *Creole Folktales*), offers a
similar argument, maintaining that though the slave narratives he
recreates represent a symbolic form of resistance, they are not
revolutionary texts. The Creole tale:

[S]platters the dominant system of values with all the immoral – or,
rather, amoral – guile of the poor and downtrodden. Yet these stories
contain no 'revolutionary' message, and their remedies for misfortune
are not collective ones. The hero is alone, and selfishly preoccupied
with saving his own skin. And so we might conclude, as Edouard
Glissant suggests, that what we have here is an *emblematic detour*, a
system of counter-values, or a counterculture, that reveals itself as
both powerless to achieve complete freedom and fiercely determined
to strive for it nonetheless.

(Chamoiseau 1998: xii–xiii)

Chamoiseau thus recognises the potential political and cultural
power of the folk tale as an expression of dissent, but avoids over-
estimating the capacity, or even the will, of the traditional storyteller
to bring about political change.

Jack Zipes, one of the preeminent analysts of fairy tales writing
in the twentieth and early twenty-first century, has offered what
remains the most complex and nuanced version of the Marxist
argument about fairy tale. For Zipes, it is impossible to assess the
political functions of folk and fairy tales, without simultaneously

assessing how they are being used in specific contexts and to specific ends. 'Folk and fairy tales remain an essential force in our cultural heritage,' Zipes argues, but: '[t]heir value depends on how we actively produce and receive them in forms of social interaction which lead toward the creation of greater individual autonomy' (Zipes 2002: 199). In their folk contexts, Zipes believes, 'folklore forms, particularly folktales, are contradictory in themselves in that they often retain and negate their utopian potential' (Zipes 1984: 331): they have a predisposition towards projecting radical and transformatory hopes for individual and social change; but at the same time they exhibit a 'conservative feudal ideology' that can be profoundly illiberal, especially where women and minority groups are concerned (Zipes 2002: 154). To further complicate the scenario, when these already 'contradictory folktales' become 'historically *appropriated* by the middle classes' after the Middle Ages and developed into 'a new literary genre, the fairy tale (*Kunstmärchen*)' they become even more conflicted, because their new literate, bourgeois mediators have worked to both deprive 'the original creators of their voice' and to instil 'the new form with a revolutionary and utopian character of its own' (Zipes 1984: 331). The only way in which we can appreciate the ways in which power is both consolidated and renegotiated in such tales, is, therefore, to attain a developed understanding of the contexts in which each narrative has functioned in the past, of the ways in which it is being utilised in the present, and of the ways in which it might be utilised in the future. Fairy tale, for Zipes, thus remains a narrative form that resists easy generalisation when it comes to the attribution of cultural and political function.

Despite Zipes's insistence on the need to understand the function of folk and fairy tales in context, however, he nonetheless identifies two features of folk and fairy tales that, in his view, remain constant through all historical periods and all cultural contexts, and that may, therefore, be regarded as universal characteristics of the genre. The first is that folk and fairy tales have their 'roots in the experience and fantasy of primitive peoples who cultivated the tale in an oral tradition' (Zipes 2002: xi). This, for Zipes, remains true even for literary fairy tales, which perpetuate the spirit of 'original folk tales' despite significant departures from the folk tale in form and subject matter (Zipes 2002: xi). The second enduring feature of the fairy tale, for Zipes, is that they are rooted in an impulse to imagine a better world: that 'all serious tales' contain a 'utopian kernel, their truth' that gives them the capacity – even if it is not realised or acted upon – to be socially transformative (Zipes 1984: 332). 'The original autonomous power of the folk tales, their aura ... has been carried over into the fairy tales,' Zipes writes, and this 'aura' is characterised by the social impulse 'to celebrate humankind's capacity to transform the mundane into the utopian as part of a communal project' (Zipes 2002: xiii). In the twentieth century, Zipes maintains, 'this fantastic projection of ... utopian impulses has been cast under the magic spell of commodity production' and so 'the original magic of the tales has itself been transformed' (Zipes 2002: xiii). Instead of offering messages of revolutionary hope, fairy-tale fantasy has been used increasingly by the culture industry to compensate for, but not to offer remedies from, social injustices and lack of individual autonomy. If radical literary criticism can break the spell of this commodity production by helping us to find other ways of realising the meaning of fairy tales, however, it will be discovered that the tales retain the revolutionary power, the 'liberating magic', that was given to them at their point of origin through 'the immediacy of the common people's perspective' (Zipes 2002: xii and 156). Even now, therefore, when folk and fairy tales, like all products of the imagination, are becoming increasingly 'instrumentalised and commercialised', folk and fairy tale remain narratives capable of conveying 'the hope of self-transformation and a better world':

> They can harbour and cultivate the germs of subversion and offer people hope in their resistance to all forms of oppression and in their pursuit of more meaningful modes of life and communication.
>
> (Zipes 2002: 21)

Scholars critical of Zipes have, on the basis of such arguments, continued to warn against the tendency of recent Marxist criticism to identify the fairy tale as a narrative form that is innately utopian and anti-authoritarian (Richardson 2009: 46–48; Limón 1983,

1984; Jones 1982: 240–44). Zipes, in turn, has responded to criticism by insisting that, whilst he sees fairy tales as narratives that always have the potential to be liberating because they 'have tended to project other and better worlds', he also recognises that the liberating potential of these other worlds is not actualised in all situations, and in some cases is actively obscured or misdirected (Zipes 2002: 3).

IDEOLOGY AND THE CONTEMPORARY FAIRY TALE

'[T]he task of Marxist research,' according to Zipes, 'is to understand the socioeconomic matrix in which all forms of culture are produced in an ideological manner' (Zipes 1984: 334). This involves an effort to grasp, on the one hand, 'how the formation of a culture industry affects the consciousness of groups and individuals', and on the other 'the ways and means by which groups and individuals rebel against ideological manipulation and develop alternatives to the manufactured and homogenised norms in Western society' (Zipes 1984: 334). In fairy-tale studies, this critical approach, whether shaped directly by Marxist theory or more indirectly by Foucauldian discourse analysis, has resulted in a two-pronged form of investigation: the critic seeks to 'demythologise' the fairy tale by exposing its complicity with hegemonic power; she also seeks to recuperate the fairy tale by revealing it to be a form of human creative expression that has the capacity to be resistant to, or critical of, dominant ideological interests. This dual approach is exemplified in Sandra Gilbert and Susan Gubar's reading of 'Snow White' in their groundbreaking examination of representations of gender in nineteenth-century European culture, *The Madwoman in the Attic* (1979). Investigating the Grimms' version of 'Snow White' in the *Kinder- und Hausmärchen*, and Disney's 1937 film adaptation *Snow White and the Seven Dwarfs*, Gilbert and Gubar argue that both the Grimm text and the Disney film work in the interests of patriarchy to divide women into two contrasting character types that may be set in competition with one another and so ruled more effectively. Snow White is the model of a 'good woman', seen from a patriarchal point of view, who is meek, passive, obedient to command and willing to do housework. '[I]n her absolute chastity, her frozen innocence, her sweet nullity' she embodies the idea of the 'angel in the house of myth' (Gilbert and Gubar 2000: 39). The Wicked Queen is her polar opposite and her murderous enemy: 'a plotter, a plot-maker, a schemer, a witch, an artist, an impersonator, a woman of almost infinite creative energy, witty, wily, and self-absorbed as all artists traditionally are' (38–39). Both women fulfil these roles under the surveillance of patriarchy, represented in the story firstly by the absent king 'for whose attentions ... the two women are battling in a feminized Oedipal struggle', and latterly by 'the voice of the looking glass, the patriarchal voice of judgement that rules the Queen's – and every woman's – self-evaluation' (37–38). The judgement that this patriarchal observer makes upon them determines their identity in the tale: Snow White is the good woman because she is subservient to the male order; she waits passively for her prince to come (so passively that at one point she appears to be dead) and may thus be handed without complaint from absent father to whom she is obedient, to the care of the male dwarfs, to the possession of the rescuing prince. The Wicked Queen, by contrast, usurps the role of male authority, endeavours to command phallic power by ordering the huntsman to kill Snow White, and takes upon herself the powers of active creation. Their rewards and punishments follow accordingly: the Queen, in the Grimm story, is forced to dance to death in red-hot shoes, and Snow White marries – or rather is married by – the Prince. Snow White's victory is pyrrhic, however. Despite the promise of the happy ending, the logic of the tale suggests that there is an 'after' to the 'happy ever' that seriously qualifies the projected happiness:

When her Prince becomes a King and she becomes a Queen what will her life be like? Trained to domesticity by her dwarf instructors, will she sit in the window, gazing out on the wild forest of her past, and sigh, and sew, and prick her finger, and conceive a child white as snow, red as blood, black as ebony wood? Surely, fairest of them all, Snow White has exchanged one glass coffin for another, delivered from the prison where the Queen put her only to be imprisoned in the looking glass from which the King's voice speaks daily. There is, after all, no female model for her in this tale except the 'good' (dead) mother and her living avatar the 'bad' mother. And if Snow White escaped her first glass coffin by her goodness, her passivity and docility, her only escape from her second glass coffin, the imprisoning mirror, must evidently be through 'badness,' through plots and stories, duplicitous schemes, wild dreams, fierce fictions, mad impersonations. The cycle of her fate seems inexorable ...

(Gilbert and Gubar 2000: 42)

In the above analysis the findings of psychoanalysis play a crucial role. Psychoanalysis helps show that the texts with which Gilbert and Gubar deal (Grimm and Disney) do not only operate at an overt level, but work to convey ideas, to inculcate behavioural patterns, at a deep level, beneath immediate conscious perception. It also helps Gilbert and Gubar to analyse the relations between protagonists, hence they cite Bettelheim's observation that the story of Snow White and the Wicked Queen is one of Oedipal conflict. At the same time, however, Gilbert and Gubar insist that the latent meanings of these stories do not reflect timeless facts about human identity, but ideological arguments that are socially produced and then reinforced through such fictions as fairy tales. Psychoanalysis, in this respect, becomes not a means of unlocking timeless realities of identity from the narratives, but a means of understanding the ways in which the dominant narratives of a culture work to construct identity. The direction of effect, for the psychoanalytic understanding of the tale, is therefore reversed as we move from Bettelheim to Gilbert and Gubar. According to Bettelheim, the fairy tale, at the latent level, shows how things are, and so helps the hearer of the tale assimilate herself into the world in which she lives. According to Gilbert and Gubar, by contrast, fairy tales offer models of how culture wants its hearers to be, and so helps socialise them into conforming to certain kinds of behaviour. This reversal of effect also means that the function of fairy-tale criticism is very different in the hands of each writer. Bettelheim's criticism presents itself as a passive reflection of what the fairy tale 'really means' and so demands nothing but understanding and acceptance from the reader. Gilbert and Gubar's criticism actively intervenes in the meaning of the tale, with the objective of challenging and transforming the reader's perceptions of it. Theirs, in this sense, is a revolutionary criticism. It seeks to demystify the fairy tale: to reveal how power operates through the narrative, and, in revealing it, to expose and contest that construction of power. It also seeks to reinterpret the fairy tale: to transform our attitudes to the narrative, and, in so doing, to encourage us to reconsider what the tale is capable of doing. Thus where Bettelheim censors the Wicked Queen's narcissism, Gilbert and Gubar read the tale against the grain by encouraging the understanding that the Queen's narcissism is 'necessitated by a state from which all outward prospects have been removed'. And thus where Grimm and Disney want readers and viewers to conclude that the 'active' female identity represented by the Queen is monstrous and the 'passive' female identity represented by Snow White is natural, Gilbert and Gubar encourage a revisionist interpretation in which the Queen's inventiveness and artistry become life affirming and Snow White's cadaverous passivity revolting.

This simultaneous endeavour to critique the cultural objectives of dominant versions of fairy tales whilst opening up new uses for fairy-tale magic, has become one of the foremost characteristics of creative responses to fairy tales in literature, film, fine art and visual culture in recent years. The literary pioneer of this approach was Angela Carter in her collection of ten short stories based on fairy tales, *The Bloody Chamber* (Carter 1979), a work that both exposes misogynist elements in conventional fairy tales, and, at the same time, uses some of 'the liberating magic that fairy tale has at its disposal' to express alternative models of gendered identity and gender relations. This artistic practice, moreover, has continued in literature and other media, producing a distinctive generation (or, perhaps now, two generations) of fairy-tale makers, committed to exploring new possibilities for fairy tales, and to adapting the fairy tale into a form capable of expressing diverse models for society and identity. In literature, this generation includes Tanith Lee (1983), Margaret Atwood (1983, 1993), Jeanette Winterson (1987, 1989), Salman Rushdie (1991, 2010a), A. S. Byatt (1994), Emma Donoghue (1997), Francesca Lia Block (2000), Kelly Link (2001, 2005), Susanna Clarke (2007), Toby Litt (2007), Danielle

Wood (2008) and Kate Bernheimer (2010) (for analysis see Zipes 1986; Bacchilega 1997; Harries 2001; Benson 2003, 2008; and McAra and Calvin 2011). New writing that draws on fairy tale is also substantially represented in Kate Bernheimer's anthology *My Mother She Killed Me, My Father He Ate Me* (Bernheimer 2011), and in her two collections of essays by various authors, *Mirror, Mirror on the Wall: Women Writers Explore Their Favourite Fairy Tales* (Bernheimer 2002) and *Brothers and Beasts: An Anthology of Men on Fairy Tales* (Bernheimer 2008), both of which seek to present fairy tales more affirmatively than has become conventional in criticism, as narratives that are capable of validating diverse forms of gendered and sexual identity. In film, the new vogue for fairy-tale making may also be seen in operation in the work of Jacques Demy, Neil Jordan, Jan Svankmajer, Hayao Miyazaki and Guillermo del Toro (see Warner 1993 and Zipes 2011). In the visual arts too fairy tales have been extensively reinterpreted. The artist Paula Rego in etchings such as *Him* (1996), and in her series of six pastel drawings *The Little Red Riding Hood Suite* (2003), develops an alternative illustrative tradition in which the power relations between the wolf and the female figures in 'Little Red Riding Hood' are interrogated and transformed, while Kiki Smith in her sculptures *Daughter* (1999), *Rapture* (2001) and *Born* (2002) contests conventional ideas of femininity in fairy tales by blurring the boundaries between beast and beauty (see Bonner 2006; see also Smith and Posner 2001). Salman Rushdie and Anish Kapoor, as a final example, have collaborated on a sculpture, *Blood Relations* (2006), in which misogynist and racist elements in the tradition of the *Arabian Nights* are exposed and satirised in order that the tradition can be reclaimed for new and more socially and artistically enabling uses (see Rushdie 2009). This contemporary vogue for revisiting fairy tales is, in many respects, distinctively of its time: it responds to a postmodern aesthetic practice of self-consciously revisiting existing genres in order to parody, pastiche and transform them; it is also informed by the imperative, voiced by equal rights activists since the 1960s, of interrogating existing cultural models to determine how these models have shaped identity in the past, and how they might be reshaped according to different paradigms in the future (see Zipes 1986 and Haase 2004). In other respects, however, the practice employed by contemporary fairy-tale writers is in continuity with an impulse that has always motivated the composition of fairy tales: to take an established model and renew it, to use the magic of transformation to generate new possibilities for art, to take the irreverence of fairy tale as a dynamic popular form and use it to batter at the gates of conformity and sterility. Carter and her successors, in this respect, though they have transformed the fairy tale for a new era, have done so under the licence of fairy tale itself, using the dialogical and polyphonic characteristics of the form, to reshape it again for new uses.

CONCLUSION

Between 1937 and the present, Walt Disney and, following his death in 1966, the Walt Disney Company, have produced nine feature films directly modelled on fairy tales: *Snow White and the Seven Dwarfs* (1937), *Cinderella* (1950), *Sleeping Beauty* (1959), *The Little Mermaid* (1989), *Beauty and the Beast* (1991), *Aladdin* (1992), *Enchanted* (2007), *The Princess and the Frog* (2009) and *Tangled* (2010). These films reflect changing tastes and attitudes in American culture over the past 70 years, and so cannot be described as homogenous in style or in social message. In *Beauty and the Beast*, scripted by Linda Woolverton, the company acknowledged feminist criticism of its representation of women in earlier films, and presented its heroine Belle as self-sufficient and intellectually curious (though her curiosity extends only to romance, and she remains a zealous individualist with a pathological hostility to common men and women). Likewise in *The Princess and the Frog*, Disney has signalled its commitment to producing more affirmative images of racial diversity by presenting its first African-American princess. Despite these gestures towards changing attitudes, however, which invariably come safely after public opinion has already shifted, the Disney model has remained remarkably consistent: the politics of the films are uniformly conservative, favouring establishment values and existing social hierarchies; success for Disney protagonists is achieved by becoming part of an elite and by leaving the lower social orders behind (unless they come with you as servants, magical or otherwise); humour is in no way transgressive, risqué or transformatory; animation is cute, clean and uncomplicated; plots are wrapped up in a tidy happy ending, and the overall effect is unthreatening and consolatory. As Jack Zipes argues, Disney's fairy-tale films consistently 'impose a vision of life ... on viewers that delude[s] audiences into believing that power can and should be entrusted only to those members of elite groups fit to administer society' (Zipes 2011: 23). All the Disney fairy-tale films:

> [F]ollow conventional principles of technical and aesthetic organization to celebrate stereotypical gender and power relations and to foster a world view of harmony. The images, words, music, and movement lead to a totalizing spectacle that basically glorifies how technology can be used to aestheticize social and political relations according to the dominant mode of production and ruling groups.
>
> (Zipes 2011: 23)

Whilst Disney has dominated the market in fairy-tale-influenced films in the last 70 years, it has not maintained an absolute monopoly over the representation of fairy tale on film. Just nine years after Disney's first feature-length animated fairy-tale film, *Snow White and the Seven Dwarfs*, released in 1937, the French director Jean Cocteau issued his film version of the Beauty and the Beast story, *La Belle et la Bête*, which counters the emergent Disney model on a number of levels. In place of Disney's compulsion for neat endings and clean moralities, Cocteau offers ambiguity, mystery and irresolution; instead of Disney's docile Snow White who bakes pies whilst waiting patiently for her prince to come, we meet the enigmatic Belle who sees in the beast an alternative to a conventional bourgeois match; and in place of Disney's conservative valorisation of establishment values, Cocteau delivers a powerful, reflective commentary on the dehumanisation of France during Nazi occupation and on its capacity to rehumanise itself in the post-war era. Cocteau's film, moreover, is just one of a range of films produced throughout the period of Disney's ascendancy by filmmakers such as Jacques Demy, Hayao Miyazaki, Jan Svankmajer, Tim Burton, Guillermo del Toro and others that make a qualitatively different use of the fairy tale on screen (see Warner 1993 and Zipes 2011). To give just three examples: Jacques Demy's ironic and self-conscious film about a father's incestuous desire for his daughter, *Donkey Skin* (1970), offers a depiction of a more dynamic and resistant heroine than was being made available in Disney films of the period. More recently, Miyazaki's free reworking of the 'Little Mermaid' story, *Ponyo* (2008), departs significantly from what Zipes describes as Disney's 'stupid pubescent musical' about 'the spunk and illusions of a spoiled princess' (Zipes 2011: 108), and uses the narrative instead to give shape to a warning about the impact upon the ocean of ecological irresponsibility. Finally, by no means exhaustively, Guillermo del Toro's masterwork, *Pan's Labyrinth* (2006), rejects the syrupy romance associated with the tradition of fairy-tale films, and offers in its place a profound exploration of the functions and value of imaginative thought and imaginative literature in the face of appalling misuses of power (see Orme 2010; Kotecki 2010). These films do not seek to delude, console or pacify audiences; rather they use the fairy tale, as it has often been used in literature, as a tool of social critique, and as a vehicle for the transformation of perceptions.

In the introduction to this study, I identified the plurality of fairy tale as the source of one of the intellectual challenges involved in studying the genre. In the modern period, the character of this plurality has changed. The fairy tale no longer exists in the developed world as a dialogic oral form, and the mass marketing of fairy-tale imagery by companies such as Disney has served to homogenise international perceptions of fairy tale on a scale previously inconceivable. As the films cited above suggest, however, and as is also suggested by the numerous revisions of the fairy tale in other media, the fairy tale remains plural in its applications in the contemporary period, and shows no signs of artistic stagnation. Artists, filmmakers and writers continue to test the dominant models by telling old stories in new ways; and fairy tales, as a result, continue to reflect the diverse views of society and self. In this process lies the enduring vitality of the fairy tale; a vitality that will persist so long as old tales stir the creative impulse to say: 'it's a well-worn tale, I've heard it before, I know how it goes; but I'll tell it again, and this time, I'll tell it in my own way'.

GLOSSARY

archetype: According to Jung, archetypes are primordial images or dispositions that have no contents in themselves, and that cannot be known by the conscious mind, but that are repeatedly manifested in concrete forms in products of the human creative imagination. Examples of archetypes include 'the great mother', the 'trickster', and 'the hero'. Because these images are derived from the collective unconscious (q.v.), which is common to all men and women, they are regarded by Jungians as universal and trans-historical; they 'are not disseminated only by tradition, language and migration, but ... can rearise spontaneously, at any time, at any place, and without any outside influence' (Jung 2003: 12). Fairy tales are an especially rich source of archetypal imagery, Jung argues, because they are 'spontaneous, naïve, and uncontrived [products] of the psyche' and, as such, 'cannot very well express anything except what the psyche actually is'. In 'fairytales, as in dreams,' Jung writes, 'the psyche tells its own story' (113).

binary opposition: A pair of conjoined terms or concepts that are defined by opposition to one another (i.e. 'good' and 'evil', 'on' and 'off'). Where one term in the binary is privileged, the opposition becomes a hierarchy. Thus, in the opposition 'virgin and whore', 'virgin' would generally be the privileged term. Such oppositions play a crucial role in the structuring of language and in human thought more generally, but as structuralist and post-structuralist theorists have demonstrated, they often express cultural values rather than natural states of affairs. Traditional fairy tales often present binary oppositions in stark forms (maiden/witch, good/evil, hero/villain), and, more often than not, reinforce the conventional hierarchies that such terms imply. In response, counter-cultural fairy tales will often seek to invert or undermine the binary oppositions to be found in conventional fairy tales, and, in so doing, to contest the cultural assumptions implied by them. Emma Donoghue's story collection *Kissing the Witch*, for instance (Donaghue 1997), works to re-privilege the figure of the witch in the fairy tale, and in so doing to reject the demonisation of certain forms of female identity that has been enacted under the guise of the good woman/bad woman polarisation.

carnivalesque: The carnivalesque is a literary mode that draws upon the energies of popular street culture to subvert authority and contest sober conventions. It is characterised by comic exuberance, bawdy and grotesque imagery, the inversion of established hierarchies, the use of fantasy to see the world in surprising new ways, and an irreverent attitude to authority. Mikhail Bakhtin in *Rabelais and His World* (Bakhtin 1965) derives the term from the period of carnival feasting before the abstinence of Lent during which the lower orders of Medieval and Renaissance society were temporarily released from the rules and conventions that bound them in everyday life. Fairy tales frequently incorporate characteristics of the carnivalesque such as marvellous transformation, the subversion or overturning of conventional oppositions (male/female, human/beast), and irreverent satire. In a more general sense, fairy tale as a genre has also been considered inherently carnivalesque because it derives from popular culture, and is therefore notionally opposed to the 'high seriousness' of established artistic forms.

cautionary tale: Cautionary tales are short prose narratives which, in Maria Tatar's definition, 'aim to mold behaviour by illustrating in elaborate detail the dire consequences of deviant conduct' (Tatar 1992: 25). Most cautionary tales do not begin life as moral warnings, in Tatar's view, but are transformed into them as writers and collectors adapt traditional folk narratives into pedagogical materials for the nursery. The best-known cautionary tale is Charles Perrault's 'Little Red Riding Hood', in which a young girl's failure to heed the warnings of her mother results in her being devoured by a wolf.

collective unconscious: The collective unconscious, according to Jung, lies at a 'deeper level' than the purely personal unconscious, and 'constitutes a common psychic substrate of a suprapersonal nature which is present in every one of us' (Jung 2003: 2). Myths and fairy tales, Jung argues, represent concretised, or conscious, manifestations of 'archetypes' (q.v.) in the collective unconscious, and so may be said to embody images that are innate, inborn, preconscious and known instinctively 'to all men' (2).

comparative method: Comparative analysis of folk or fairy tale involves the cross-referencing of different versions of a narrative type or narrative element. Often, the different versions of a narrative that are compared will derive from diverse historical periods or geographical locations, and the object of the analysis will be to explore how a particular story has modified across time and space. The kinds of judgement that are made using the comparative method will depend upon the scholar's predisposition. Some scholars use comparative science to make judgements about where myths, folk tales and fairy tales originally came from; some to make judgements about the cultural and ideological significance of narrative transformations. Major comparativists include the Brothers Grimm, Max Müller, and the 'historic-geographic' scholars of the Finnish school. Collections such as Maria Tatar's *Classic Fairy Tales* (Tatar 1999), which places diverse versions of a narrative type side by side, are also comparative in spirit.

demythologisation: In the sense meant by Roland Barthes, a mythology is a kind of discourse that is presented as natural and a-historical, but that is in fact conditioned by history and society (Barthes 1972: 109–11). Demythologisation is the process by which a mythology which is presented as natural is exposed as a social construct that has particular designs upon its audience.

diachronic and synchronic: Diachronic refers to development over time, synchronic to the nature of a phenomenon at any one time.

Euhemerism: The belief that myths and folk tales are a form of disguised or misremembered history. In the fourth century BCE, the Greek philosopher Euhemerus of Messene, in his *Sacred Document*, proposed that the Gods of Greek mythology had originally been real men, whose deeds had been of sufficient renown that they had, over time, become transformed into mythical figures. In later centuries, this 'Euhemerist' position has been adopted by numerous scholars of myth and fable, including, influentially, the preeminent mythographer of eighteenth-century Europe, the Abbé Antoine Banier (1673–1741). Modern Euhemerism has departed from these earlier formulations in several respects. Inflected by Marxist cultural materialism, it has become increasingly less concerned with the idea that myths and fables originate in historical events, and more concerned with discovering how popular traditional stories reflect the cultural realities of the societies that have shaped them. Modern Euhemerism has also become less preoccupied with the lives of the powerful and heroic, and more attentive to the ways in which the experiences of common men and women may be said to breathe through popular tales (see Röhrich 1991 and Darnton 2001).

folklore: Popular cultural materials and cultural practices that have the power to persist in tradition. The English term 'folklore' was introduced by the British civil servant and amateur antiquarian William John Thoms in a letter to the popular nineteenth-century journal *The Athenaeum,* published on 22 August 1846. Writing pseudonymously as Ambrose Merton, Thoms proposed that those materials that, in England, were usually designated 'Popular Antiquities or Popular Literature' – 'manners, customs, observances, superstitions, ballads, proverbs' – should be renamed: 'Popular' should be replaced by 'folk' and 'literature' should be replaced by 'lore' to create what Thoms regarded as a good 'Saxon' compound 'Folk-Lore – *the Lore of the people*' (Dundes 1999: 11).

folkloristics: The study of folklore.

folk tale: The folk tale is a short, popular narrative that either circulates orally in tradition, or that has at some point of its history circulated orally. It characteristically deals with peasant protagonists in the familiar settings of town and countryside and it depicts these protagonists triumphing over adversity through some clever ruse or some extraordinary stroke of luck, or, if they are not sufficiently quick-witted or sufficiently lucky, suffering the penalties of their idiocy.

frame story: The frame story provides a pretext and a context for the diverse acts of narration that take place within a story collection. Typically, the frame story will initiate a collection by explaining how the acts of storytelling came about, and by introducing the narrator (or narrators) of the stories. Frame stories will also often conclude a collection, explaining how the events that initiated the collection are resolved, or simply providing a terminal point for a set of fictions. In some instances, too, the frame story will be used to provide linking episodes or interludes between narratives. Numerous ancient story collections have frame stories, including, most influentially, the Middle Eastern collection *The Thousand and One Nights* which begins by describing how it comes about that Scheherazade must tell stories to Prince Shariyar each night in order to save her own life. The framed story collection became popular in Europe in the Early Modern period, as exemplified by Boccaccio's *Decameron* and Basile's *Pentamerone*.

hypertextuality (hypertext and hypotext): According to Gérard Genette in *Palimpsests*, the term 'hypertextuality' describes 'any relationship uniting a text B ... to an earlier text A ... upon which it is grafted in a manner that is not that of commentary' (Genette 1997: 5). In this intertextual relationship, Text B is described as the 'hypertext', and Text A the 'hypotext'. Thus in Angela Carter's reworking of 'Beauty and the Beast', 'The Courtship of Mr Lyon', Carter's short story is the 'hypertext' and the tradition of 'Beauty and the Beast' forms one of the story's 'hypotexts'. It will be noted, however, that the 'hypotext' is not a singular or a stable 'source' in the traditional sense: Carter takes her notions of 'Beauty and the Beast' from a number of places, including de Beaumont's 'La Belle et la Bête', Jean Cocteau's film of the same name, her own childhood recollections of the story, and so on. Carter's ideas of 'Beauty and The Beast' are also likely to have been shaped by any number of additional cultural influences, including illustrations, picture books, advertisements, cartoons, etc. The 'hypotext' thus constitutes a complex of cultural influences that have come to shape the idea of 'Beauty and the Beast' that Carter is responding to, and that Carter's own contribution has further transformed.

intertextuality: Intertextuality refers to the ways in which texts (novels, stories, poems, films, etc.) depend for their meaning upon other texts. It is a particularly apposite term in the study of fairy tale, since each iteration of a fairy tale necessarily develops from and responds to a complex idea of that tale as it has been created in existing works of literature, film, visual culture, oral culture and so on. Intertextuality, as a critical term, offers a more accurate description of the relationship between fairy tales and tradition than the more conventional model of 'fiction' and 'source', since it allows us to understand the web of textuality from which each fairy tale emerges as manifold and shifting (see also **hypertextuality**).

latent and manifest content: In Freudian psychoanalytic theory, these terms are used to describe two levels of content apparent in dreams. The manifest contents of the dream are the events recalled by the dreamer (the overt content); latent content refers to the systems of meaning and significance that the analyst believes to be at work 'beneath' the surface, which are driven by unconscious or repressed motives. The interpretation of dreams, Freud argued, involves the extraction of its latent content; a process that occurs through discussions between patient and analyst during which the particular meanings of a dream's symbolism for a patient are explored. Analysts of fairy tale influenced by Freud's work on dreams claim, similarly, that the fairy tale can also be seen as an imaginative text that has both a manifest content (what happens in the story) and a latent content (what the story 'actually means'). Frequently, this claim is also coupled by the assertion that those elements in a fairy tale's 'manifest' content which seem inexplicable and bizarre will become explicable once the underlying psychological logic of the fairy tale has been understood.

manifest content: See **latent and manifest content**.

morphology: The study of forms. In biology, a morphological study involves the examination of the component parts of an organism, and the ways in which these component parts relate to one another and to the whole. Vladimir Propp in *The Morphology of the Folktale* borrows this scientific language in his endeavour to assert that there can also be a science of the study of forms in literature. A 'morphology' of the fairy tale, for Propp is: 'a description of the tale according to its component parts and the relationship of these component parts to each other and to the whole' (Propp 1968: 19).

motif: Stith Thompson defines a motif as 'the smallest element in a tale having a power to persist in tradition' (Thompson 1977: 415). Motifs are common story elements, or basic units of narrative, that frequently appear in stories of different types. Hence, the 'motif' of the 'forbidden chamber' (classified by Thompson as Motif C611), which appears in Perrault's 'Bluebeard', may also be found, in variant form, in the quite different stories 'The Virgin Mary's Child' and 'Faithful Johannes' by the Brothers Grimm. In his monumental *Motif Index of Folk-Literature* compiled between 1932 and 1936 (revised and enlarged 1955–58), Thompson assembles an extensive list of the motifs to be found in folk narrative, and has supplied each motif with an identifying code, a description and a bibliography of narratives in which it can be found.

Orientalism: In traditional terms, Orientalism refers to the study of the languages and cultures of the Orient. In his influential 1978 work *Orientalism*, however, Edward Said redefined the term to describe the ways in which ideas of the East are constructed through Western discourses. This construction of the East, Said argued, was designed to support imperial power in the region, since it reinforced the idea that the East was morally and socially inferior to the West, and so in need of civilising. Popular narrative traditions from the East have often been used by Western scholars to support Orientalist discourses about the region; *The Arabian Nights*, for instance, has frequently been used in an Orientalist manner to justify European claims for the irrationality and sensuality of Middle Eastern culture (see Kabbani 1986, 2004). Conversely, European fairy tales frequently include Orientalist stereotypes, as is evident, for instance, in the depiction of cruel and ignorant Saracens in the fairy tales of Straparola, or in certain visual depictions of Bluebeard that portray him as a Turkish sultan (see Zipes 2001: 140–42).

superorganicism: A term used by Alan Dundes to critique any theoretical methodology that takes the 'folk' out of 'folklore'. Superorganic theories have 'little or nothing to do with people', and so are insufficiently aware of the social and cultural contexts in which folk narratives circulate. (See Dundes 2007: 130.)

survivals: The term 'survivals' was coined by the Victorian anthropologist E. B. Tylor, and explored in his major work *Primitive Culture* (1871). In the nineteenth century, folklorists influenced by the anthropological work of Tylor, chief amongst them Andrew Lang, argued that the myths and household tales of Europe were the 'survivals' of primitive traditions that encoded the laws and beliefs of savage peoples. Because Lang and Tylor believed that societies pass through the same stages of development, they also argued that the savage meanings of European myths and fairy tales could best be understood by examining the ways in which myths and stories were used in the present by Australian Aboriginals and Native Americans, who Victorian anthropologists believed were at earlier phases of civilisation than Europeans. The ethnographic assumptions that underlie these theories have now been widely rejected. Lutz Röhrich, in the mid-twentieth century, defined survivals as 'rigidified elements of belief and custom which have lost their original meaning' (Röhrich 1991: 57).

symbol: In psychoanalytic theory, symbols are generally understood to be produced when one idea or image is substituted for another as a result of an unconscious process. 'By symbol we mean a substitute for something we are not conscious of, for a repressed unconscious concept,' writes Géza Róheim (1992: 5). Traditional fairy tales are often seen by psychoanalytic critics to be narratives that contain symbols of this sort. In more general parlance, a symbol is an image or idea that, whether for conscious or unconscious reasons, represents something else, either because it has comparable qualities, or because it has come to represent that thing by custom or convention.

synchronic: See **diachronic and synchronic**.

tale type: The abstracted type of a story that can be found in multiple versions in diverse regions and at diverse historical times. Thus the basic narrative of 'Cinderella', of which thousands of versions have been collected, is an international tale type. The 'type' itself has no independent existence since the story only exists in multiple variants, though some scholars (notably those of the historic-geographic school) have argued that the more a story conforms to its typical form, the closest it is to the original story. Ultimately, a tale type is best understood as a sort of distillation or abstraction of the story, rendered in skeletal form, and is not dissimilar from a Platonic 'form' or Aristotelian 'essence'. The types of the folk tale have been indexed by Hans-Jörg Uther in *The Types of International Folktales: A Classification and Bibliography* (Uther 2004). Uther's index is a reworked and updated version of the tale type index first compiled by Antti Aarne in 1910, translated and expanded by the American scholar Stith Thompson in 1928 (*The Types of the Folktale*; second revision, 1961). In citations of tale types, ATU stands for Aarne/Thompson/Uther, and the number supplied after the prefix indicates where the description and bibliographic citation for this particular tale can be found in the Index. A classification system has also been developed for migratory legends by Reidar Thoralf Christiansen (see Christiansen 1958). Tale types in this index are classified with the prefix ML.

BIBLIOGRAPHY

Andersen, Hans Christian (2002 [1865]) *Stories and Tales*, trans. Henry William Dulcken, London: Routledge.

——(2004) *Fairy Tales*, trans. Tiina Nunnally, ed. Jackie Wullschlager, London: Penguin.

Anderson, Graham (2000) *Fairytale in the Ancient World*, London: Routledge.

Atwood, Margaret (1983) *Bluebeard's Egg*, Toronto: McClelland and Stewart.

——(1993) *The Robber Bride*, Toronto: McClelland and Stewart.

Bacchilega, Cristina (1997) *Postmodern Fairy Tales: Gender and Narrative Strategies*, Philadelphia: University of Pennsylvania Press.

Bakhtin, Mikhail (1984 [1965]) *Rabelais and His World*, trans. Hélène Iswolsky, Bloomington: Indiana University Press.

Baldwin, William (1988 [c.1560]) *Beware the Cat*, ed. William A. Ringler and Michael Flachmann, San Marino: Huntington.

Barchilon, Jacques and Peter Flinders (1981) *Charles Perrault*, Twayne's World Authors, Boston: Twayne.

Barthes, Roland (1972 [1957]) *Mythologies*, trans. Annette Lavers, New York: Hill and Wang.

Bascom, William R. (1981) *Contributions to Folkloristics*, Meerut: Folklore Institute.

Basile, Giambattista (2007) *The Tale of Tales, or Entertainment for Little Ones*, trans. Nancy Canepa, Detroit: Wayne State University Press.

Beckwith, Martha Warren (1924) *Jamaica Anansi Stories*, New York: American Folk-Lore Society.

Benjamin, Walter (1999) *Illuminations*, trans. Harry Zohn, ed. Hannah Arendt, London: Pimlico.

Benson, Stephen (2003) *Cycles of Influence: Fiction, Folktale, Theory*, Detroit: Wayne State University Press.

——(ed.) (2008) *Contemporary Fiction and the Fairy Tale*, Detroit: Wayne State University Press.

Bernheimer, Kate (ed.) (2002) *Mirror, Mirror on the Wall: Women Writers Explore Their Favourite Fairy Tales*, New York: Anchor.

——(ed.) (2008) *Brothers and Beasts: An Anthology of Men on Fairy Tales*, Detroit: Wayne State University Press.

——(2010) *Horse, Flower, Bird: Stories*, Minneapolis: Coffee House Press.

——(ed.) (2011) *My Mother She Killed Me, My Father He Ate Me*, London: Penguin.

Bettelheim, Bruno (1978 [1976]) *The Uses of Enchantment: The Meaning and Importance of Fairy Tales*, London: Penguin.

Block, Francesca Lia (2000) *The Rose and the Beast: Fairy Tales Retold*, New York: Joanna Cotler.

Boccaccio, Giovanni (1995) *The Decameron*, trans. G. H. McWilliam, London: Penguin.

Bonner, Sarah (2006) 'Visualising Little Red Riding Hood', in *Moveable Type* 2, available at www.ucl.ac.uk/english/graduate/issue/2/sarah.htm (accessed 9 November 2012)

Bottigheimer, Ruth (2002) *Fairy Godfather: Straparola, Venice and the Fairy Tale Tradition*, Philadelphia: University of Pennsylvania Press.

——(2009) *Fairy Tales: A New History*, New York: State University of New York Press.

Brathwaite, Kamau (1970) *Folk Culture of the Slaves in Jamaica*, Port of Spain: New Beacon.

——(1977) *Wars of Respect: Nanny and Sam Sharpe and the Struggle for People's Liberation*, Kingston, Jamaica: API.

Brennan, Catherine (2003) 'Anna Walter Thomas and the Power of Privilege', in *Angers, Fantasies and Ghostly Fears: Nineteenth Century Women from Wales and English-Language Poetry*, Cardiff: University of Wales Press, pp. 170–203.

Briggs, Katharine M. (ed.) (1970–71) *A Dictionary of British Folk-Tales in the English Language*, 2 parts, 4 vols, London: Routledge.

——(2002) *The Fairies in Tradition and Literature*, London: Routledge.

Buchan, David (1990) 'Folk Literature', in *Encyclopedia of Literature and Criticism*, ed. Martin Coyle *et al.*, London: Routledge, pp. 976–90.

Byatt, A. S. (1994) *The Djinn in the Nightingale's Eye: Five Fairy Stories*, London: Chatto.

Campbell, Joseph (1993 [1949]) *The Hero With a Thousand Faces*, London: Fontana.

Canepa, Nancy (ed.) (1997) *Out of the Woods: The Origins of the Literary Fairy Tale in Italy and France*, Detroit: Wayne State University Press.

——(1999) *From Court to Forest: Giambattista Basile's Lo cunto de li cunti and the Birth of the Literary Fairy Tale*, Detroit: Wayne State University Press.

——(2007) 'Introduction', *Giambattista Basile's The Tale of Tales, or Entertainment for Little Ones*, trans. Nancy Canepa, Detroit: Wayne State University Press, pp. 1–31.

Carter, Angela (1991) 'Introduction', *The Virago Book of Fairy Tales*, ed. Angela Carter, London: Virago, pp. ix–xxii.

——(1997) *Shaking a Leg: Collected Journalism and Writings*, ed. Jenny Uglow, London: Chatto and Windus.

——(1998 [1979]) *The Bloody Chamber and Other Stories*, London: Vintage.

Chamoiseau, Patrick (1998) *Strange Words*, trans. Linda Coverdale, London: Granta.

Christiansen, Reidar Thoralf (1958) *The Migratory Legends: A Proposed List of Types with a Systematic Catalogue of the Norwegian Variants*, FF Communications 175–6, Helsinki: Suomalainen Tiedeakatemia Academia Scientiarum Fennica.

Clarke, Susanna (2007 [2006]) *The Ladies of Grace Adieu and Other Stories*, London: Bloomsbury.

Clodd, Edward (1898) *Tom Tit Tot: An Essay on Savage Philosophy in Folk Tale*, London: Duckworth.

Cox, Marian Roalfe (1893) *Cinderella: Three Hundred and Forty-Five Variants*, London: David Nutt.

Cuddon, J. A. (1992) *Dictionary of Literary Terms and Literary Theory*, 3rd edn, London: Penguin.

Darnton, Robert (2001 [1984]) 'Peasants Tell Tales: The Meaning of Mother Goose', in *The Great Cat Massacre, and Other Episodes in Cultural History*, London: Penguin, pp. 9–72.

de Jean, Joan (1991) *Tender Geographies: Women and the Origins of the Novel in France*, New York: Columbia University Press.

Delarue, Paul (1989) 'The Story of Grandmother', in *Little Red Riding Hood: A Casebook*, ed. Alan Dundes, Wisconsin: Garland, pp. 16–20.

Donaldson, Julia (Author) and Axel Scheffler (Illustrator) (1999) *The Gruffalo*, London: Macmillan.

Donoghue, Emma (1997) *Kissing the Witch*, London: Penguin.

Dorson, Richard (1968) *The British Folklorists: A History*, London: Routledge.

Dundes, Alan (ed.) (1989) *Little Red Riding Hood: A Casebook*, Wisconsin: Garland.

——(ed.) (1999) *International Folkloristics: Classic Contributions by the Founders of Folklore*, Lanham: Rowman and Littlefield.

——(2007) *The Meaning of Folklore: The Analytical Essays of Alan Dundes*, ed. Simon J. Bronner, Logan: Utah State University Press.

Ellis, John M. (1983) *One Fairy Story Too Many: The Brothers Grimm and Their Tales*, Chicago: University of Chicago Press.

Fison, Lois A. (ed.) (1899) *Merry Suffolk: Master Archie and Other Tales*, London: Jarrold and Sons.

Freud, Sigmund (1958a [1913]) 'The Occurrence in Dreams of Material from Fairy Tales', in *Complete Psychological Works*, ed. James Strachey, vol. 12, London: Hogarth Press, pp. 279–87.

——(1958b [1913]) 'The Theme of the Three Caskets', in *Complete Psychological Works*, ed. James Strachey, vol. 12, London: Hogarth Press, pp. 289–301.

Fromm, Erich (1957 [1951]) *The Forgotten Language: An Introduction to the Understanding of Dreams, Fairy Tales and Myths*, New York: Grove Press.

Genette, Gérard (1997) *Palimpsests: Literature in the Second Degree*, trans. Channa Newman and Claude Dubinsky, Nebraska: University of Nebraska Press.

Georges, Robert A. and Michael Owen Jones (1995) *Folkloristics: An Introduction*, Bloomington: Indiana University Press.

Gerould, Gordon (1908) *The Grateful Dead: The History of a Folk Story*, London: David Nutt.

Gilbert, Sandra M. and Susan Gubar (2000) *The Madwoman in the Attic: The Woman Writer and the Nineteenth-Century Literary Imagination*, 2nd edn, New Haven: Yale University Press.

Godden, Rumer (2004) 'Hans Christian Andersen', in *Danish Writers from the Reformation to Decadence: 1550–1900*, ed. Marianne Stecher-Hansen, *Dictionary of Literary Biography*, vol. 300, Farmington Hills: Gale, pp. 14–41.

Goldberg, Christine (2001) 'The Composition of "Jack and the Beanstalk"', *Marvels and Tales* 15:1, pp. 11–26.

Gramsci, Antonio (1985) *Selections from Cultural Writings*, ed. David Forgacs and Geoffrey Nowell-Smith, trans. William Boelhower, London: Lawrence and Wishart.

Greimas, A. J. (1983 [1966]) *Structural Semantics: An Attempt at Method*, trans. Daniele McDowell, Ronald Schleifer, and Alan Velie, Lincoln: University of Nebraska Press.

Grimm, Jacob and Wilhelm Grimm (1992) *The Complete Fairy Tales of the Brothers Grimm*, ed. and trans, Jack Zipes, New York: Bantam.

Haase, Donald (1999) 'Yours, Mine, or Ours? Perrault, the Brothers Grimm, and the Ownership of Fairy Tales', in *The Classic Fairy Tales*, ed. Maria Tatar, New York: Norton, pp. 353–64.

——(ed.) (2004) *Fairy Tales and Feminism: New Approaches*, Detroit: Wayne State University Press.

Harries, Elizabeth Wanning (2001) *Twice Upon a Time: Women Writers and the History of the Fairy Tale*, Princeton: Princeton University Press.

Hartland, E. S. (2000 [1890]) *English Fairy and Folk Tales*, New York: Dover.

Hébert, Louis (2006) 'The Actantial Model', available at www.signosemio.com/greimas/actantial-model.asp (accessed 1 May 2011).

Hoffmann, E. T. A. (1992) *The Golden Pot and Other Tales*, trans. Ritchie Robertson, Oxford: Oxford University Press.

Hunt, Margaret (ed. and trans.) (1884) *Grimm's Household Tales, with the Author's Notes*, 2 vols, London: George Bell and Sons.

Irwin, Robert (1994) *The Arabian Nights: A Companion*, London: Penguin.

Jacobs, Joseph (1890) *English Fairy Tales*, London: David Nutt.

——(1891) 'Childe Rowland', *Folk-Lore* 2:2, pp. 182–97.

——(1893) 'The Folk', *Folk-Lore* 4:2, pp. 233–38.

——(1894) *More English Fairy Tales*, London: David Nutt.

Jameson, Fredric (2002) *The Political Unconscious: Narrative as a Socially Symbolic Act*, London: Routledge.

Jones, Ernest (1951) 'Psycho-Analysis and Folklore', *Essays in Applied Psychoanalysis*, vol. 2, London: Hogarth, pp. 1–21.

Jones, Steven Swann (1982) 'Review of *Breaking the Magic Spell: Radical Theories of Folk and Fairy Tales*, by Jack Zipes', *Western Folklore* 41, pp. 240–44.

——(2002) *Fairy Tales: The Magic Mirror of Imagination*, New York: Routledge.

Jung, Carl Gustav (2003) *Four Archetypes: Mother, Rebirth, Spirit, Trickster*, trans. R. F. C. Hull, London: Routledge.

Kabbani, Rana (1986) *Europe's Myths of Orient*, Basingstoke: Macmillan.

——(2004) 'The Arabian Nights as an Orientalist Text', in *The Arabian Nights Encyclopedia*, ed. Ulrich Marzolph and Richard Van Leeuwen, Santa Barbara: ABC-CLIO, pp. 25–29.

Kamenetsky, Christa (1992) *The Brothers Grimm and their Critics*, Athens: Ohio University Press.

Kotecki, Kristine (2010) 'Approximating the Hypertextual, Replicating the Metafictional: Textual and Sociopolitical Authority in Guillermo del Toro's *Pan's Labyrinth*', *Marvels and Tales* 24:2, pp. 235–54.

Krebs, Albin (1971) 'Louis Armstrong, Jazz Trumpeter and Singer, Dies', Obituary, *The New York Times*, 7 July, reprinted at www.nytimes.com/learning/general/onthisday/bday/0804.html (accessed 1 May 2012).

Lamb, Mary Ellen (2006) *The Popular Culture of Shakespeare, Spenser, and Jonson*, London: Routledge.

Lang, Andrew (1884a) *Custom and Myth*, London: Longmans, Green and Co.

——(1884b) 'Household Tales; Their Origin, Diffusion, and Relations to the Higher Myths', in *Grimm's Household Tales, with the Author's Notes*, ed. and trans. Margaret Hunt, 2 vols, London: George Bell and Sons, pp. xi–lxx.

——(1888) 'Introduction', *Perrault's Popular Tales*, ed. Andrew Lang, Oxford: Clarendon, pp. vii–cxv.

——(1913 [1899]) *Myth, Ritual and Religion*, 2nd edn, 2 vols, London: Longmans, Green and Co.

Lee, Tanith (1983) *Red as Blood: Or, Tales from the Sisters Grimmer*, New York: Daw.

Lévi-Strauss, Claude (1984) 'Structure and Form: Reflections on a Work by Vladimir Propp', trans. Monique Layton, in *Theory and History of Folklore* by Vladimir Propp, ed. Anatoly Liberman, Minneapolis: University of Minnesota Press, pp. 167–88.

Limón, José E. (1983) 'Western Marxism and Folklore: A Critical Introduction', *The Journal of American Folklore* 96:379, pp. 34–52.

——(1984) 'Western Marxism and Folklore: A Critical Reintroduction', *The Journal of American Folklore* 97:385, pp. 337–44.

Link, Kelly (2001) *Stranger Things Happen*, Northampton, MA: Small Beer Press.

——(2005) *Magic For Beginners*, Northampton, MA: Small Beer Press.

Litt, Toby (2007) *Hospital*, London: Hamish Hamilton.

Luke, David (1982) 'Introduction', to *Selected Tales* by Jacob Grimm and Wilhelm Grimm, ed. and trans. David Luke, London: Penguin, pp. 9–43.

Lüthi, Max (1976) *Once Upon a Time: On the Nature of Fairy Tales*, trans. Lee Chadeayne and Paul Gottwald, Bloomington: Indiana University Press.

——(1986) *The European Folktale: Form and Nature*, trans. John D. Niles, Bloomington: Indiana University Press.

MacDonald, George (1999) *The Complete Fairy Tales*, ed. U. C. Knoepflmacher, London: Penguin.

Malinowski, Bronislaw (1926) *Myth in Primitive Psychology*, London: Kegan Paul.

Mayhew, Henry (1864) *London Labour and the London Poor*, London: Charles Griffin.

McAra, Catriona and David Calvin (2011) *Anti-Tales: The Uses of Disenchantment*, Cambridge: Cambridge Scholars.

McCrum, Robert (2004) 'Where the Gruffalo Roams: Interview with Julia Donaldson', *The Observer*, 29 August, reprinted at www.guardian.co.uk/books/2004/aug/29/booksforchildrenandteenagers.features (accessed 1 July 2011).

McGlathery, James, (ed.) (1988) *The Brothers Grimm and Folktale*, Urbana: University of Illinois Press.

Michaelis-Jena, Ruth (1970) *The Brothers Grimm*, London: Routledge.

Morrison, Toni (1997 [1987]) *Beloved*, London: Vintage.

Müller, Max (1872) *Chips from a German Workshop: Essays on Mythology, Traditions, and Customs*, vol. 2, New York: Charles Scribner.

Oinas, Felix J. (1978) 'The Political Uses and Themes of Folklore in the Soviet Union', in *Folklore, Nationalism and Politics*, ed. Felix J. Oinas, Columbus, Ohio: Slavica.

Opie, Iona and Peter Opie (eds) (1980) *The Classic Fairy Tales*, London: Oxford University Press.

Orenstein, Catherine (2002) *Little Red Riding Hood Uncloaked*, New York: Basic Books.

Orme, Jennifer (2010) 'Narrative Desire and Disobedience in *Pan's Labyrinth*', *Marvels and Tales* 24:2, pp. 219–34.

Philip, Neil (1992) *The Penguin Book of English Folktales*, London: Penguin.

Pickering, Samuel F. (1981) *John Locke and Children's Books in Eighteenth Century England*, Knoxville: University of Tennessee Press.

Plato (1925) *Lysis, Symposium, Gorgias*, trans. W. R. M. Lamb, Loeb Classical Library 166, Cambridge, Mass.: Harvard University Press.

——(1953) *The Republic*, in *The Dialogues of Plato*, trans. B. Jowett, 4th edn, vol. 2, Oxford: Clarendon.

Prince, Alison (1998) *Hans Christian Andersen: The Fan Dancer*, London: Allison and Busby.

Propp, Vladimir (1968) *The Morphology of the Folktale*, trans. Laurence Scott, ed. Louis A. Wagner, 2nd edn, American Folklore Society, Austin: University of Texas Press.

Pullman, Philip (1995) *Northern Lights*, London: Scholastic.

Purkiss, Diane (2000) *Troublesome Things: A History of Fairies and Fairy Tales*, London: Penguin.

Richardson, Alan (2009) 'Wordsworth, Fairy Tales and the Politics of Children's Reading', in *Romanticism and Children's Literature in Nineteenth-Century England*, ed. James Holt McGavran, Athens: University of Georgia Press, pp. 34–53.

Robb, Graham (2004) 'Fairy Tales', in *Strangers: Homosexual Love in the Nineteenth Century*, New York: Norton, pp. 197–222.

Roberts, Warren E. (1995 [1958]) *The Tale of the Kind and Unkind Girls: AA – TH 480*, Detroit: Wayne State University Press.

Róheim, Géza (1992) *Fire in the Dragon and Other Psychoanalytic Essays on Folklore*, ed. Alan Dundes, Princeton: Princeton University Press.

Röhrich, Lutz (1991) *Folktales and Reality*, trans. Peter Tokofsky, Bloomington: Indiana University Press.

Rölleke, Heinz (1988) 'New Results of Research on Grimms' Fairy Tales', in *The Brothers Grimm and Folktale*, ed. James McGlathery, Urbana: University of Illinois Press, pp. 101–11.

Rosenberg, Bruce A. (1991) *Folklore and Literature: Rival Siblings*, Knoxville: University of Tennessee Press.

Rushdie, Salman (1991 [1990]) *Haroun and the Sea of Stories*, London: Granta.

——(2009 [2006]) 'Blood Relations – An Interrogation of Arabian Nights', at http://fabrica.org.uk/exhibitions/exhibition-archive/blood-relations/blood-relations-further-reading-2/ (accessed 24 July 2012)

——(2010a) *Luka and the Fire of Life*, London: Jonathan Cape.

——(2010b) 'Salman Rushdie on *Luka and the Fire of Life*', available at www.amazon.com/Luka-Fire-Life-SalmanRushdie/dp/0679463364/ref=sr_1_1?ie=UTF8&qid=1301491769&sr=8–1 (accessed 30 March 2011).

Seifert, Lewis (1996) *Fairy Tales, Sexuality and Gender in France 1690–1715: Nostalgic Utopias*, Cambridge: Cambridge University Press.

Silver, Carol (1999) *Strange and Secret Peoples: Fairies and the Victorian Consciousness*, Oxford: Oxford University Press.

Small, Ian (1994) 'Introduction', to *Complete Short Fiction* by Oscar Wilde, ed. Ian Small, London: Penguin, pp. vii–xxvii.

Smith, Kiki and Helaine Posner (2001) *Telling Tales*, New York: International Centre of Photography.

Snyder, Louis L. (1978) 'Cultural Nationalism: The Grimm Brothers' Fairy Tales', in *The Roots of German Nationalism*, Bloomington: Indiana University Press, pp. 35–54.

Somadeva, Bhatta (1968) *The Ocean of Story*, trans. C. H. Tawney, ed. N. M. Penzer, 10 vols, Delhi: Motilal Banarsidass.

Straparola, Giovan Francesco (1894) *The Nights of Straparola*, trans. W.G Waters, 2 vols, London: Lawrence and Bullen.

Szumsky, Brian (1999) 'The House That Jack Built: Empire and Ideology in Nineteenth-Century British Versions of "Jack and the Beanstalk"', *Marvels and Tales* 13.1, pp. 11–30.

Tatar, Maria (1992) *Off With Their Heads! Fairy Tales and the Culture of Childhood*, Princeton: Princeton University Press.

——(ed.) (1999) *The Classic Fairy Tales*, New York: Norton.

——(2003) *The Hard Fact of the Grimms' Fairy Tales*, 2nd edn, Princeton: Princeton University Press.

——(2006) *Secrets Beyond the Door: The Story of Bluebeard and His Wives*, Princeton: Princeton University Press.

Teverson, Andrew (2010) 'Giants Have Trampled the Earth: Colonialism and the English Tale in Samuel Selvon's *Turn Again Tiger*', *Marvels and Tales* 24.2, pp. 199–218.

Thompson, Stith (1952) *The Star-Husband Tale*, Oslo: Studia Septentrionalia IV.

——(1977) *The Folktale*, Berkeley: University of California Press.

Todorov, Tzvetan (1975) *The Fantastic: A Structural Approach to a Literary Genre*, trans. Richard Howard, Ithaca: Cornell University Press.

Tolkien, J. R. R. (1964) *Tree and Leaf*, London: Unwin.

Uther, Hans-Jörg (2004) *The Types of International Folktales*, 3 parts, FF Communications 284, Helsinki: Suomalainen Tiedeakatemia Academia Scientiarum Fennica.

von Franz, Marie-Louise (1996) *The Interpretation of Fairy Tales*, revised edn, Boston: Shambhala.

Walter Thomas, Anna (1898) 'Tom-Tit-Tot' (Letter), *The Times*, 31 October, p. 14.

Warner, Marina (1993) 'The Uses of Enchantment', in *Cinema and the Realms of Enchantment*, ed. Duncan Petrie, London: BFI.

——(1994) *Managing Monsters: Six Myths of Our Time*, The Reith Lectures, London: Vintage.

——(1995) *From the Beast to the Blonde: On Fairy Tales and Their Tellers*, London: Vintage.

Watson, Jeanie (2009) '"The Raven: A Christmas Poem": Coleridge and the Fairy Tale Controversy', in *Romanticism and Children's Literature in Nineteenth-Century England*, ed. James Holt McGavran, Athens: University of Georgia Press, pp. 14–33.

Wilde, Oscar (1994) *Complete Short Fiction*, ed. Ian Small, London: Penguin.

Williams, W. Glynn (n.d. [1922]) *Memoir of Mrs. Anna Walter Thomas*, Holywell: W. Williams and Son.

Wilson, William A. (1973) 'Herder, Folklore and Romantic Nationalism', *Journal of Popular Culture* 6:4, pp. 819–35.

Winterson, Jeanette (1987) *The Passion*, London: Bloomsbury.

——(1989) *Sexing the Cherry*, London: Bloomsbury.

Wood, Danielle (2008) *Rosie Little's Cautionary Tales for Girls*, Melbourne: Orion.

Wordsworth, William (1994) *Selected Poems*, ed. John O. Hayden, London: Penguin.

Wullschlager, Jackie (2001) *Hans Christian Andersen: The Life of a Storyteller*, London: Penguin.

Zipes, Jack (1983) *Fairy Tales and the Art of Subversion: The Classical Genre for Children and the Process of Civilisation*, London: Heinemann.

——(1984) 'Folklore Research and Western Marxism: A Critical Replay', *The Journal of American Folklore* 97:385, pp. 329–37.

——(ed.) (1986) *Don't Bet on the Prince: Contemporary Feminist Fairy Tales in North America and England*, Aldershot: Gower.

——(ed. and trans.) (1989) *Beauties, Beasts and Enchantments: Classic French Fairy Tales*, New York: Penguin.

——(ed. and trans.) (1992) *The Complete Fairy Tales of the Brothers Grimm*, New York: Bantam.

——(ed.) (1993) *The Trials and Tribulations of Little Red Riding Hood*, 2nd edn, New York: Routledge.

——(1997) *Happily Ever After: Fairy Tales, Children and the Culture Industry*, New York: Routledge.

——(ed.) (2000) *The Oxford Companion to Fairy Tales*, Oxford: Oxford University Press.

——(ed.) (2001) *The Great Fairy Tale Tradition: From Straparola and Basile to the Brothers Grimm*, New York: Norton.

——(2002) *Breaking the Magic Spell: Radical Theories of Folk and Fairy Tales*, revised and expanded, Lexington: University Press of Kentucky.

——(2007) *When Dreams Came True: Classical Fairy Tales and Their Tradition*, 2nd edn, London: Routledge.

——(2011) *The Enchanted Screen: The Unknown History of Fairy Tale Films*, London: Routledge.

INDEX

Aarne, Antti 20, 26, 97–99, 151
Adorno, Theodor 128
Aesop 23
Afanás'ev, Aleksander 72, 99–100, 103
African tales 22, 126
'Aladdin' 73, 140
allegory 6, 23–24, 26
Anansi stories 22
Andersen, Hans Christian 8, 32, 37, 43, 71–82, 118; 'Aunty Toothache' 81–82; 'The Emperor's New Clothes' 74; 'Little Claus and Big Claus' 74, 76; 'Little Ida's Flowers' 74–75, 76; 'The Little Match Girl' 73–74; 'The Little Mermaid' 77, 78, 79, 80–81, 118; 'The Naughty Boy' 76; 'The Princess and the Pea' 74, 76–77; 'The Red Shoes' 79–80; 'The Snow Queen' 79, 80; 'Thumbelina' 75; 'The Tinderbox' 74, 76
Anglo Saxon literature 43
animal tales 20, 21, 22–23, 44
animals 29, 93, 94 see also wolves
anthropology 5, 16, 31, 89, 92–96, 104, 105, 130, 150
anthropomorphism 22, 92, 102
antiquarianism 85–86, 147
Arabian Nights, The see Thousand and One Nights, The
archetypes 34, 35, 111, 116–17, 121, 123, 144, 145
aristocracy 42, 46, 51, 52–56, 60, 61–62, 65, 71, 80
Armstrong, Louis 10, 15
Arnim, Achim von 62, 63–64, 66
Aryan race 90–92, 94
Asbjørnsen, Peter 72
Assyrian empire 43
Atwood, Margaret 137

Aubrey, John 85–86
Australia 11, 14, 22, 150
authenticity 36–37, 41–42, 62, 68–71, 122
autobiography in fairy tale 51, 73, 80–81, 118

Babylonian civilization 43
Bacchilega, Cristina 138
Bakhtin, Mikhail 145
Baldwin, William 13
Banier, Antoine 146
Barbauld, Mrs. 86
Baroque, the 36, 49
Barthes, Roland 129, 146
Bascom, William 16, 130
Basile, Giambattista 8, 31, 36, 42, 43, 45–51, 147; 'Cagliuso' 51; 'Corvetto' 47–48; 'The Goose' 49–50; 'Petrosinella' 43; 'The Seven Pieces of Bacon Rind' 43; 'Sun, Moon and Talia' 43, 50–51
'Beauty and the Beast' 23, 47, 59–60, 141, 148
Beckwith, Martha Warren 14
Benjamin, Walter 128, 129–30
Benson, Stephen 107, 108, 138
Bernard, Catherine 52, 58
Bernheimer, Kate 32, 138
Bettelheim, Bruno 6, 110, 114, 117–23, 136–37
binary opposition 105–6, 135, 144
bisexuality 80–81, 118
Bloch, Ernst 129–30
Block, Francesca Lia 137
'Bluebeard' see under Perrault, Charles
Boccaccio, Giovanni: The Decameron 28, 44–45, 46, 147
Bökendorf circle 65
Book of Tobit 43

Bottigheimer, Ruth 35, 47, 49
bourgeoisie *see* middle classes
bowdlerisation of stories 4, 67–68,
    120–21
Brathwaite, Kamau 126–27
Brémond, Claude 106
Brennan, Catherine 41
Brentano, Clemens 49, 62, 63–64, 66
Brer Rabbit 22
Briggs, Katharine 21, 26, 28
Brix, Hans 80
büchmärchen (use of term) 31
Burton, Tim 142
Byatt, A. S. 32, 137
Byron, George Gordon 76

Cabinet des fées, Le 61
Campbell, Joseph 34, 35, 117
Canepa, Nancy 44, 45, 47, 49, 51
'Cap o' Rushes' 28, 39, 40
capitalism 128–30
Caribbean tradition 22, 126–27, 131
carnival 46, 49, 50, 130–31, 145
Carroll, Lewis: *Alice's Adventures in
    Wonderland* 73, 76, 78
Carter, Angela 32, 37, 49, 80, 82, 126,
    137–39, 148; *The Bloody Chamber*
    137, 148; 'The Courtship of Mr Lyon'
    148; 'Puss in Boots' 49
censorship 120–21
Chamoiseau, Patrick: *Strange Words*
    126, 131
chapbooks 14, 22, 85, 122
Chase, Richard: *The Jack Tales* 14
Chaucer, Geoffrey: *The Canterbury
    Tales* 28
children: association of fairy tales with
    49, 53, 58, 59–60, 119, 128;
    depictions of 25, 57, 66, 68, 74–75,
    79–80, 112–13, 119–20, 125;
    education of 38, 59–60, 66, 75, 76,
    78, 84–86, 127, 129; literature for 2,
    3, 14, 24–25, 49, 53, 57, 58, 59–60,
    66, 67, 74–81, 85–86, 119;
    psychological development of

119–20; storytelling for 38, 57, 74–75,
    83–85, 129
chivalry 43, 44, 45
'Cinderella' 28, 39, 57, 58, 85, 102, 107,
    114–15, 125, 140, 151
cinema *see* film
Clarke, Susanna 40–41, 137
class (social) 11–12, 14–15, 41–42,
    65–66, 68–69, 69–70, 71, 84, 126,
    127–30 *see also specific classes*
classical literature 23, 43, 83–84
'Clever Jack' 18, 19, 20, 29
Clodd, Edward 39–41
Cocteau, Jean: *Beauty and the Beast*
    141–42, 148
Coleridge, Samuel Taylor 86–87;
    The Lyrical Ballads 87
collective unconscious 5, 34, 111, 116–17,
    144, 145 *see also* the unconscious
Collin, Edvard 73, 81
colonialism *see* imperialism
communism 127–28
comparative method, the 89, 91,
    97–98, 125, 145–46
contemporary fairy tales 3, 9, 32,
    40–41, 49, 79, 134–39, 142–43
countercultural tales 49, 130, 131,
    137–39, 141, 144–45
countryside 11–12, 17, 69, 87
court (aristocratic) 42, 43, 46, 47–48,
    51–53, 61–62
Cox, George 92–93
Cox, Marian Roalfe 108
Creole tales 131
Croker, Thomas Crofton 72
culture industry 129, 133, 134
cumulative tales 22, 24–25, 66
Cupid and Psyche 114

d'Aulnoy, Marie-Catherine 8, 30, 36, 37,
    52–56, 58, 62, 67; 'Beauty with the
    Golden Hair' 53; 'The Blue Bird' 55–56;
    'The Good Little Mouse' 56; 'The
    Island of Happiness' 52, 53; 'The
    White Cat' 55; 'The Yellow Dwarf' 55

d'Auneuil, Louise 53
Darnton, Robert 3, 4, 110, 122, 124–26, 130–31, 147
de Beaumont, Jeanne-Marie Leprince 59–60, 148
del Toro, Guillermo 138, 142
Delarue, Paul 3, 4, 125
Demy, Jacques: *Donkey Skin* 138, 142
demythologisation 134, 146
Denmark 73, 77
Dickens, Charles 74
didacticism 6, 23–24, 30, 57, 59–60, 75, 84–86
diffusion of tales 12–15, 89–90, 94–95, 96–97
Disney, Walt 51, 134–37, 140–42; *Beauty and the Beast*, 140; *The Little Mermaid* 142; *The Princess and the Frog*, 140; *Snow White and the Seven Dwarfs* 134–37
Donaldson, Julia: *The Gruffalo* 25
'Donkey Skin' *see under* Perrault, Charles
Donoghue, Emma: *Kissing the Witch* 32, 137, 144–45
dreams 111–15, 116, 144, 148–49
Droste-Hülshoff, Jenny von 65
Dundes, Alan 3, 27, 101, 107–8, 110, 150
dwarfs 55, 112–13, 135

Early Modern period 8, 26, 44–51, 84, 145, 147–48
Egyptian tales 43
Ellis, John M. 36, 69–71, 91
empire *see* imperialism
English tradition 14, 21, 22, 24, 25–26, 28, 29, 30–31, 38–41, 43, 62, 85–87, 147
Enlightenment, the 8, 51, 61, 84–86, 96, 125–26
Erasmus, Desiderius 84
escapism 19, 47–48
euhemerism 126, 146–47 *see also* historical interpretation
exempla 21, 59

explanatory tales 23
Expressionism 82

fable 21, 22–23, 44, 57, 146
fairies 21, 22, 25–26, 31, 50, 52, 53, 57
fascism *see* Nazism
feminism 6, 8, 18–19, 52, 80, 126, 134–39, 141
Fielding, Sarah: *The Governess* 30
film 3, 9, 14, 134–37, 138, 140–42, 148
Finnish school 97–98, 146
Fiorentino, Giovanni: *Il Pecorone* 45
'Fisherman and His Wife, The' *see under* Grimm, Jacob and Wilhelm
'Fleeing Pancake, The' 24
Folk-Lore (journal) 39
folk, the (concept of) 8, 10–12, 36, 42, 49, 58, 71, 72, 116, 122
food in fairy tale 125–26
Force, Charlotte-Rose de la 36, 52
formalism 98–108
formula tales 21, 24–25
frame tales 46, 147
Frankfurt School Marxism 128
French tales 2–4, 8, 30, 48–49, 51–60, 61–62, 69, 106, 122, 124–26, 141–42
Freud, Sigmund 29, 96, 109–18, 148–49
'Frog King, The' *see under* Grimm, Jacob and Wilhelm
Fromm, Erich 122

Galland, Antoine: *Les mille et une nuits* 59
gender 103, 134, 137, 138, 141 *see also* masculinity; women in fairy tales
Genette, Gérard 148
Gennep, Arnold van 34–35
Georges, Robert 15
German tales 2, 5, 11, 15, 31, 38, 49, 61–71, 87–89, 90–91, 95, 118
Gilbert, Sandra: *The Madwoman in the Attic* 110, 134–37
'Gingerbread Man, The' 24
Glissant, Edouard 131

Goethe, Johann Wolfgang von 62
Gorky, Maxim 128–29
gothic, the 29–30, 32
Gramsci, Antonio 128
'Grateful Dead, The' 43
Greimas, A.-J. 106
Grimm, Jacob and Wilhelm 5, 8, 35,
    36–37, 62–71, 72, 82; assembly of
    the *Kinder-und Hausmärchen* 63–66,
    68–71; 'The Boy who Went Forth to
    Discover Fear' 26–27, 129; 'The
    Brave Little Tailor' 64; classification
    of tales 15, 17, 30–32, 21–22, 'Clever
    Else' 66; 'The Clever Farmer's
    Daughter' 66; contributors to the
    collection 63, 64–66, 68, 71;
    feminist approaches to the tales
    134–37; 'The Fisherman and His
    Wife' 17–18, 20, 63, 64; as folklore
    scholars 83, 87–89; 146; as forgers
    69–71; 'The Frog King' 87–89, 92,
    93, 95, 117; and German
    Romanticism 62–63, 72, 87; 'The
    Goose Girl' 65; 'Hans My
    Hedgehog' 65; 'Hansel and Gretel'
    49, 66, 67–68; 'How Some Children
    Played at Slaughtering' 66–67;
    influence of Italian tales on 9;
    'The Juniper Tree' 66; 'Little Red
    Cap' 2, 4, 66, 67, 68, 122;
    modification of tales 36–37, 67–71;
    as nationalists 62–63, 90–91;
    peasant sources of tales 11, 42,
    65–66, 69–71; psychoanalytical
    approaches to 117, 118; 'Rapunzel'
    49, 64, 66; religious elements in
    the tales 23; 'The Robber
    Bridegroom' 68; 'Rumpelstiltskin'
    19, 38, 39–41, 42–43, 63, 66, 102,
    112–13; 'Snow White' 63, 66,
    134–37; and theories of folktale
    origins 90–91; 'The Three Feathers'
    117; 'The Three Golden Hairs of
    the Devil' 117; 'The Three Spinners'
    19–20

Grimm, Herman 68
Grimm, Ludwig 65, 67
grotesque, the 42, 49–50, 145
Gubar, Susan: *The Madwoman in the
    Attic* 110, 134–37

Haase, Donald 123, 139
'Hansel and Gretel' *see under* Grimm,
    Jacob and Wilhelm
Hard Candy 3
Harries, Elizabeth Wanning 25, 36–37,
    57, 58, 138
Hartland, E. S. 121–22
Hassenpflug family 64: Jeanette 63;
    Marie 2, 68–69
Haxthausen family, von 65, 66; August
    65; Ludowine 65; Werner 65
Herder, Johann Gottfried von 62, 87
heroism 16, 17, 19, 33, 53, 80, 101–2,
    106, 117
Hesse, Herman 32
historical interpretation 4–5, 6, 7–8,
    109–10, 122–27, 146–47
historic-geographic school 96–98,
    146, 151
Hoffmann, E. T. A. 32, 72, 75
hypertextuality 148 *see also*
    intertextuality

ideology 6, 91, 124, 127, 134–37
illustration *see* visual arts
imperialism 118, 123, 149–50
independent invention 89, 94–95
indexes of folktales 20–21, 98, 149, 151
Indian origin, theory of 90
Indian tradition 14, 23, 43, 44, 92
Indo-European language theory 90–93
inheritance 125
instructional tale *see* didacticism
intertextuality 8–9, 148
Irish tales 22, 72
Italian tales 5, 8, 44–51

'Jack and the Beanstalk' 13–14, 119–20,
    122–23

Jacobs, Joseph 11–12, 14, 22, 24, 39–40, 121–22
Jamaican tradition 14, 126
James, Henry 29–30
Jameson, Fredric 102
jocular tales 20–21, 26–27
jokes *see* jocular tales
Jones, Ernest 114, 117
Jones, Michael Owen 15
Jones, Steven Swann 29, 32
Jordan, Neil 138
Jung, Carl Gustav 34, 35, 109–11, 116–17, 144, 145,

Kabbani, Rana 59, 150
Kapoor, Anish 138
Karadžić, Vuk Stefanović 72
Kathasaritsagara see Ocean of Story, The
Keats, John: 'La belle dame sans merci' 26
'King of the Cats, The' 13–14
Kipling, Rudyard: *Just So Stories* 23
Knaben Wunderhorn, Des 62, 63
Krause, Johann Friedrich 64
Krohn, Kaarle 97
kunstmärchen 31–32, 36–37, 132

Ladybird books 25
Lamb, Charles 86
Lamb, Mary Ellen 84
Lang, Andrew 92–97, 107; *The Gold of Fairnilee* 73
latent content 5–6, 7, 96, 109–10, 111, 148–49
Lee, Tanith 32, 137
legend 13, 15–16, 21–22, 26, 62, 151
Lévi-Strauss, Claude 104–6
Lewis, C. S. 79
Lhéritier, Marie-Jeanne 36, 43, 52, 58
Limón, José 127–28
Link, Kelly 32, 137
literary fairy tale *see kunstmärchen*
Litt, Toby 137
Little Goody Two-Shoes, The History of 85

'Little Mermaid, The' 77, 78, 79, 80–81, 118, 140, 142
'Little Red Riding Hood' 1–6, 57, 58, 66, 67, 114, 122, 138, 145
Locke, John 85
Lönnrot, Elias: *The Kalevala* 72
Louis XIV 51, 54, 57
love 52, 53, 55–56, 81, 115
Lowth, William 84
Lüthi, Max 24, 33–34, 35

MacDonald, George 32, 73, 78; *Adela Cathcart* 72–73
Macpherson, James 70–71
magic 18, 21, 28, 29–30, 32–33, 45, 47, 93, 96, 119–20, 129, 133, 137, 139
Mailly, Jean de 52
Maintenon, Madame de 54
Malinowski, Bronislaw 16
manifest content 114, 115–16, 148–49
Manuel, Infante don Juan 74
märchen (use of term) 31–32
marriage 52, 55–56, 59–60, 88, 95, 101, 111–12, 135
Marxism 6, 18, 127–34, 146–47
masculinity 53, 60, 84, 119–20, 122–23, 135
Mayer, Charles-Joseph de 61
Mayhew, Henry: *London Labour and the London Poor* 18
Medieval period 43, 74, 145
men in fairy tales *see* masculinity
middle classes 4, 18, 41–42, 45, 50, 59–60, 65, 69–71, 132, 141
Middle East, the 44, 59, 147, 150
migration (of peoples) 69, 90, 95, 144
Millien, Achille 3, 4
misogyny in fairy tales 80, 137, 138
  see also women in fairy tales
Miyazaki, Hayao 138; *Ponyo* 142
Moe, Jorgen 72
monogenesis 95
Montanus, Martinus 64
morals in fairy tales *see* didacticism
Morlini, Girolamo 45

morphological analysis 98–108, 149
Morrison, Toni 126
Mother Goose tales 57, 83
motherhood 54, 67, 68, 119–20, 120, 123, 136, 144
motifs 31, 45, 95, 98, 114, 149
Müller, Max 91–93, 95–96, 146
Munch, Edvard 82
Murat, Henriette Julie de 48–49, 53
myth: definitions of 15, 16, 17; opposed to fairy tale 16, 17, 19, 21, 129; as sources of fairy tales 5, 89–93 see also solar mythology; demythologisation

Nashe, Thomas 84
nationalism 41, 42, 62–63, 70, 72, 90–91, 126–27
Native American tales 97, 101, 105, 150
nature myths 91–93
Nazism 91, 141–42
Norse saga 14, 43
Norwegian tales 72
novelle 21, 27–28, 44–47
nursery tale 21–22, 24–25

Ocean of Story, The 43
Oedipal process 119–20, 136
Oelenberg manuscript 63, 67–68
old wives' tales 83–86
Olrik, Axel 17, 35
oral tradition 3–4, 8, 11–15, 35, 38–42, 65, 85–86, 120, 125, 126–27, 132–33, 142, 147
Orenstein, Catherine 3
orientalism 59, 149–50
Ossian 70

Panchatantra, The 23
pantomime 14
papyrus (Egyptian) 43
parody 14, 27, 59, 138
patriarchy 6, 18–19, 56, 58, 68, 95, 103, 125, 134–37
peasantry see working classes

Peele, George: The Old Wife's Tale 43
Perceforest 43
Percy, Thomas: Reliques of Ancient English Poetry 62
Perrault, Charles 8, 31, 35–37, 42, 49, 52, 56–58, 59, 61, 125; 'Bluebeard' 57, 58, 67, 149; 'Cinderella' 28, 57, 58, 125; 'Donkey Skin' 28, 52, 53–54, 142; 'The Fairies' 57; 'The Foolish Wishes' 52; 'Grisélidis' 52; 'Little Red Riding Hood' 2–4, 57, 122, 145; 'Little Thumbling' 57, 125; 'Puss in Boots' 50, 57, 67, 125; 'Riquet with the Tuft', 52, 57; 'Sleeping Beauty' 43, 50–51, 57, 58
Perrault, Pierre D'Armancour 3, 42, 57
Philip, Neil 14, 41
philology 91–93
Plato 83–84, 151
polygenesis 95
Porcelli, Bruno 45
postmodernism 137–39
Préchac, Jean de 52
primitive peoples (concept of) 5, 6, 11, 16, 39, 90, 93–96, 132, 150
Primrose Prettyface, The Renowned History of 85
Prince, Alison 76–77
Propp, Vladimir: The Morphology of the Folktale 98–107, 149
psychoanalysis: 5–6, 7, 34–35, 96, 108, 109–24, 136–37, 144, 145, 148–49, 150–51
Pullman, Philip: Northern Lights 78–79
Purkiss, Diane 26
'Puss in Boots' 45, 50–51, 49, 57, 67, 125

race (ethnicity) 91, 94, 138, 140, 150
Rackham, Arthur 82
rape 6
'Rapunzel' see under Grimm, Jacob and Wilhelm
rationalism 57–58, 75, 79, 83–87, 96, 116
Rego, Paula 138
religion 16, 17, 21, 23–24, 44, 67, 68

Renaissance *see* Early Modern period
repression 96, 111, 148–49, 150–51
rite of passage 5–6, 34–35
Roberts, Warren E. 97
Róheim, Géza 113, 114, 116, 117, 150–51
Röhrich, Lutz 7, 124, 147, 150
Rölleke, Heinz 68–69, 71
romance 43, 44, 140
Romanticism 15, 35, 36, 62–63
Rosenberg, Bruce 35
Rousseau, Jean Jacques 61
Rowling, J. K.: *Harry Potter and the Philosopher's Stone* 76
'Rumpelstiltskin' *see under* Grimm, Jacob and Wilhelm
Runge, Philipp Otto 17, 63, 64
Rushdie, Salman 137; *Blood Relations* 138; *Haroun and the Sea of Stories* 79; *Luka and the Fire of Life* 1, 7, 79
Ruskin, John: The *King of the Golden River* 72
Russian Revolution 127–28
Russian tales *see* Afanás'ev, Aleksander

Said, Edward 149–50
salon fairy tales 51–56
Sanskrit 43, 91–93
satire 47–48, 51, 53–54, 59, 74, 138, 145
savages *see* primitive peoples
Savigny, Friedrich Carl von 63
Schlegel, Friedrich 87
Schultz, Friedrich 64
schwank see jocular tales
Seifert, Lewis 36, 53, 54, 58–59
Serbian tales 72
Sévigné, Madame de 52
sex in fairy tales 27, 49, 51, 76–77, 79–81, 112–13, 117, 119–20, 120–21
sexuality 80–81, 118, 138
Shakespeare, William: 62; *King Lear* 14, 114–15; *The Merchant of Venice* 114–15; *A Midsummer Night's Dream* 26
sibling rivalry 120, 125
Silver, Carol 26
slavery 46, 97, 126–27, 131

'Sleeping Beauty' 43, 50–51, 57, 58, 140
Small, Ian 78
Smith, Kiki 138
'Snow White' 63, 66, 134–37, 140, 141
Snyder, Louis 91
socialisation through fairy tale 59–60, 134, 136; *see also* didacticism; ideology
socio-historical approaches 8, 108, 109–10, 120–39; *see also* historical interpretation
Socrates 83–84
Sokolov, J. 128
solar mythology 5, 6, 91–93
Somadeva, Bhatta 43
'Sorcerer's Apprentice, The' 46–47
Southgate, Vera 25
Soviet Union, the 127–29
Spenser, Edmund: *The Faerie Queene* 26
spinning (as work)19–20, 57, 74
Straparola, Giovan Francesco 8, 18, 45–47, 48–49
structuralism 105–8
subversion in fairy tale 129–31, 133–34, 145
superorganicism 107–8, 150
survivals 5, 12, 34, 90, 93–95, 150
Svankmajer, Jan 138, 142
symbolism 5, 7, 22, 79, 111–17, 119–20, 121–22, 150–51
Szumsky, Brian 123

Tabart, Benjamin 14
tale types 20–22, 89, 95, 97–99, 107, 151
Tatar, Maria 3, 19, 110, 120–21, 145, 146
Taylor, Edgar 31
Ténèze, Marie-Louise 125
Thackeray, William Makepeace: *The Rose and the Ring* 72
Thiele, Just Mathias 74
Thompson, Stith 20, 22, 26, 28, 97–98, 149, 151
Thoms, William John 147
Thousand and One Nights, The 28, 59, 138, 150

Tieck, Ludwig 87
Todorov, Tzvetan 29–30, 101
Tolkien, J. R. R. 31, 32; *The Lord of the Rings* 33
'Tom Thumb' 17, 57, 75, 125
'Tom Tit Tot' 22, 38–43
transmission of tales 5, 9, 11, 12–15, 35, 38–42, 43–44, 71, 89–90, 94–95, 96–98, 145–46
Travers, P. L. 79–80
trickster figure 2, 3, 6, 18, 22, 25, 57, 144
Trimmer, Sarah 85
'Two Brothers, The' 43, 66
Tylor, E. B. 150

uncanny, the 29–30
unconscious, the 34, 109–21, 144, 145, 148–49, 150–51
urban legend 26
Uther, Hans-Jörg 98, 151
utopianism 129–30, 132–34

Vedas, the 92
Victorian period 11–12, 38–42, 91–96, 122–23, 150
Viehmann, Katharina Dorothea 65–66, 69
Villeneuve, Gabrielle-Suzanne de 59
violence in fairy tales 57, 66, 79–80
visual arts 9, 137, 138, 148
von Franz, Marie-Louise 117

Walpole, Horace 29, 30
Walt Disney Company *see* Disney, Walt
Walter Thomas, Anna 38–42
Warner, Marina 9, 19, 57, 126, 138, 142
West Indies *see* Caribbean tradition; Jamaican tradition
'Whittington and His Cat' 22
Wild family 64, 69, 87; Dortchen 63, 66; Lisette 63
Wilde, Oscar 32, 78; 'The Fisherman and his Soul' 78
Wilson, William A. 91
Winterson, Jeanette 137
wish-fulfilment 18, 19–20, 112–13, 115, 130
witches 33, 68, 135, 144–45
wolves 1–3, 6, 33, 113–14, 138, 145
women in fairy tales 6, 41–42, 54–58, 80–81, 123, 126, 132, 134–38, 140–43, 144–45
Wood, Danielle 3, 137–38
Woolverton, Linda 140
Wordsworth, William 86–87; *The Lyrical Ballads* 87
work (representations of) 19–20, 125
working classes 6, 15, 36, 42, 65, 120–21, 124–26, 130–31, 147
Wullschlager, Jackie 76, 80–81, 118

Zipes, Jack 3, 44, 51, 54, 68, 110, 118, 123, 129–30, 131–34, 138, 139, 141, 142

www.routledge.com/literature

Magic(al) Realism

By Maggie Ann Bowers

Series: The New Critical Idiom

Bestselling novels by Angela Carter, Salman Rushdie, Gabriel Garcia Marquez and a multitude of others have enchanted us by blurring the lines between reality and fantasy. Their genre of writing has been variously defined as 'magic', 'magical' or 'marvellous' realism and is quickly becoming a core area of literary studies. This guide offers a first step for those wishing to consider this area in greater depth, by:

- exploring the many definitions and terms used in relation to the genre

- tracing the origins of the movement in painting and fiction

- offering an historical overview of the contexts for magic(al) realism

- providing analysis of key works of magic(al) realist fiction, film and art.

This is an essential guide for those interested in or studying one of today's most popular genres.

2004 | 160 Pages | PB: 978-0-415-26854-7 | HB: 978-0-415-26853-0

arn more at: www.routledge.com/9780415268547

Available from all good bookshops

www.routledge.com/literature

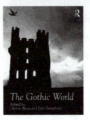